CALLINGS, COMMITMENTS, & VOCATIONAL CHALLENGES

Catherine Cronin Carotta
and Michael Carotta

TWENTY-THIRD PUBLICATIONS

185 WILLOW STREET • PO BOX 180 • MYSTIC, CT 06355
TEL: 1-800-321-0411 • FAX: 1-800-572-0788
E-MAIL: ttpubs@aol.com • www.twentythirdpublications.com

Twenty-Third Publications
A Division of Bayard
185 Willow Street
P.O. Box 180
Mystic, CT 06355
(860) 536-2611 or (800) 321-0411
www.twentythirdpublications.com
ISBN:1-58595-392-X

Library of Congress Catalog Card Number: 2004114647
Printed in the U.S.A.

Cover photo by Catherine Cronin Carotta.

Acknowledgments

This work has emerged out of experiences extended to us over the last ten years by the Teaching for Spiritual Growth Summer Institute at Boston College and the Weston Jesuit School of Theology along with the Fetzer Institute's Courage to Teach program.

We are grateful to those who supported its journey toward publication, particularly Jo Rotunno, Diane Lampitt, Bill Huebsch, and Gwen Costello.

Sincerest appreciation is extended to Dr. Sharon Daloz Parks for her willingness to support us in breaking open the research she and others compiled in the book *Common Fire: Lives Of Commitment in A Complex World* (Beacon Press, 1997).

We are very grateful for the encouragement we received over the years from our friends and colleagues in Louisville who modeled authentic vocational sensitivities daily.

We celebrate our parents, William and Yvonne Cronin and Alfred and Anne Carotta, for giving us a life of love and confidence.

Finally, this work is dedicated to those who, from all occupations, perspectives, and stages of life, remain committed to the courageous and spiritual task of fulfilling the "Promise to Become."

Contents

Introduction

*H*ow might we revisit the notion of callings, commitments, and vocational challenges in the midst of our journeys today? In what ways can a fresh embrace of these three ancient elements of life provide us with a clearer sense of purpose, a stronger sense of fulfillment, and an authentic sense of Spirit?

> Dream lofty dreams, and as you dream, so shall you become.
>
> —James Allen

The essential elements of this book were born out of Catherine Cronin Carotta's doctoral research on the spirituality of educators. The work has been expanded by Michael's seminars with people from all walks of life. The journey began with the simple question, "What is a vocation?" While our path has traversed the thoughts of the ancients and the post-moderns, our travels have always focused on exploring how each individual interprets a vocation.

This work is intended to offer reflections on how we all might sustain the Spirit fueling the direction of our lives. It is also meant to help you name what you have already discovered, shed light on what you already deal with, and push to the surface that which you already intuit.

Most of all, this book seeks to cultivate a vocational spirituality that may help you make fresh sense of the opportunities, tensions, challenges, and practices that comprise the Work of Your Life.

1

A promise to honor the true essence of your being is the sustenance for your exploration. A good and powerful question is all that is needed to begin the journey of discovering the dimensions of your vocation.

What is your dream of the "Promise to Become?"

Part 1

Vocational Callings

*H*umanity cannot forget its dreamers; it cannot let their ideals fade and die; it lives in them; it knows them as the realities which it shall one day see and know.

Composer, sculptor, painter, poet, prophet, sage, these are the makers of the after-world, the architects of heaven. The world is beautiful because they have lived; without them, laboring humanity would perish.[1]

—James Allen

a semi-retired man in his mid-60s lives in Vermont. Every day he goes to his backyard barn and paints. Time flies. He is caught up in the delight he finds in painting. When finished with a work, he quietly admires it for a few days or weeks and then pitches it, at peace with the joy of having been able to paint, with no interest in having others view his work. He then begins painting another work. "I love painting. When I paint, I feel so alive! I'm in another place. I feel like I'm exercising my deepest self. I cannot fully describe the experience of it other than to tell you that I believe it is my vocation. I'm sure of it!"

Is what this man describes *really* a vocation?

A debate ensues whenever this example is shared with a group gathered for vocational renewal. Most in the group take issue with the man's vocational assertion. "It's not a vocation for him, it's an avocation…a hobby…a passion." Others will insist that a vocation must have a dimension of helping others. "If his painting inspired others, then yes. If not, then it's his therapy, which is great, but not his vocation." Most want to assert, "Vocation, by its definition, contributes to the common good." Others suggest, "Painting gets him centered so that he can better serve those around him."

Others defend the painter's assertion, pointing out that a vocation centers around doing what is most natural for you. "A vocation is about working out of your truest self, using the gifts, talents, and pursuits that are at your deepest being." "Vocation is about the authentic exercise of who you are and how you were made, whether serving others or not." "Vocation is that place that honors the true nature of yourself. When you touch that place it enables you to act out your work and your life in a different kind of way. It allows you to take the inside you to the outside." Still others insist that the entire question is inappropriate, saying, "Who can judge another person's vocation? It's not our place. Only the individual can determine if something is a vocation."

> You are sitting in a real estate office closing an offer on a new house you are buying. After weeks of working with the real estate agent, you compliment him on the quality of his work, his integrity, good will, patience, and the generous way he has made time for you and your family's many questions, doubts, and preferences. He goes on to tell you that he has found that selling real estate really "has worked out well," that he can make his own schedule, and he enjoys helping people cope with the stress of selling their home or having to find a new home in the midst of transferring from a town they hated to leave.
>
> He explains that he used to be a high school music teacher for eleven years before moving into real estate. He talks with fondness of "moving up the ladder" from teaching music at a small school to eventually being the music teacher and award-winning band director at one of the region's biggest high schools. As he makes photocopies of your contract and all the other paperwork, you ask: "Would you say that teaching was your vocation?"

Without hesitation, he whirls around with a stack of papers in each hand and peering over the bifocals at the tip of his nose, he enthusiastically shouts, "Without question! Absolutely! Teaching was definitely my vocation. I think I was born to teach! It just became too much for me. After awhile, I couldn't keep up the pace. So I had to find something more manageable." Still nodding his head, as he turns back to the photocopier, he reasserts: "Yes, definitely, teaching was my vocation, without a doubt."

Aren't vocations more or less permanent and lifelong? Can you really find true happiness if you walk away from your vocation? The former band director turned real estate agent loves his new work. He's good at it. He's happy. He's helping others get through what psychologists claim is one of the top three stressors in modern life. But this is not his vocation. Instead, he claims that he intentionally gave up his vocation because it became "too much." And he's perfectly fine without it.

We all have assumptions about vocations, but most of us haven't taken the time to check in on these vocational assumptions. Our conversations with others have led us to the following understandings of vocation:

- Vocational callings are not necessarily permanent or lifelong.
- Vocational callings aren't completely destined or appointed "from above."
- You can be very happy without living out your occupational vocation.
- Vocational callings don't always involve serving others.
- Vocational callings may not have anything to do with work.

The way we understand vocational callings has a strong and direct influence on our ability to sustain them. For example, if you believe that vocation is about fulfillment, then you may doubt your vocational calling during times when you are not feeling fulfilled at all. If you believe that happiness cannot be fully experienced unless you are living out your vocation, your journey may be a dissatisfied and restless one, ignoring the richness of your present situation until you find the "destined" one. If you believe that a vocation must include service, then you may question your vocation during those times when you feel that people are not being well served by your efforts. If you believe that vocation is about work, then you may never see yourself as more than what your occupation says that you are.

We all have a sense that the word "vocation" relates to being called. But where do you assume the call comes from? If you believe the call comes from the transcendent voice "above," then you will listen for that call by submitting yourself to the will of the transcendent. If you believe that the call is from beyond us, you will venture out in response to the voices or desires of others. If you believe that the call comes from a voice within you, then you will listen to that call by going inward and getting to better know yourself.

Nature and Dimensions of Vocational Calls

Sometimes it takes five words
of buoyant, tensile English
to explain one ancient leathery word.[2]

Diana Der-Hovanessian

The word "vocation" has ancient lineage and is derived from the Latin word *vocare*, which means, "to call." Historically, the notion of a "call" first began with religious origins and can be traced to early Christianity, when men and women responded to a personal call from God by entering the monastic orders.[3] Today, the terms "vocation" and "calling" may be viewed in either a religious or a secular sense.

A broadening of the concept of vocation occurred during the Reformation when Martin Luther rejected the notion that vocation applied only to the clergy with his insistence that all people had vocations that could be enacted in ordinary life.[4] According to Emmet, the notion of religious vocation was supplemented by the "doctrine of the calling" in the life of all people.[5]

Further development of the concept of vocation can be seen in the Calvinist doctrine of predestination, where success in worldly endeavors was interpreted as assurance of eternal salvation. This interesting mix of success in the world in order to obtain salvation transformed the original notion of vocation from a call by God to a relationship with God, which would be confirmed by worldly success. In fact, some believe that this theology provided the crucial ideological underpinnings for the emergence of capitalism.[6]

Continued secularization of the dimensions of vocation occurred with the onset of the Industrial Revolution. The language used to describe employment began to take on such terms "work," "job," "occupation," "career," and "profession."[7] Hansen proposed that the choice of terminology may reflect the analysis by sociologists, political scientists, labor organizers, and psychologists of human, institutional, and occupational development. In addition, the term that is used may be a reflection of an individual's educational level, professionality, speciality, sense of commitment to others, or degree of spirituality.

So why is it important to talk about what we call our work? Deciding how we describe our work is more than a matter of semantics. It's about how we will put into action our description of what and who we are. According to Ian Hacking,

> People are affected by what we call them and more importantly by the available classifications within which they can describe their own actions and make their own choices. People act and decide under new descriptions and as new possibilities for description emerge, so do new kinds of action.[8]

Research on vocation reveals that there are a number of ways in which different individuals choose to view vocation. Careful examination of these views provides the grounds for further understanding of the dimensions of vocation. Review of the literature has revealed the following conceptualizations of vocation:[9]

1. Vocare means "to call" (Hansen, 1995).

2. "Vocation finds its expression at the crossroads of public obligation and personal fulfillment" (Hansen, 1995).

3. Enacting a vocation includes "the love of the drudgery it involves" (Smith, 1934).

4. Vocation is "where your deep gladness and the world's deep hunger meet" (Buechner, 1973).

5. An authentic call coming from a voice within with an invitation to honor "the nature of my true self" (Palmer, 1998).

6. Vocation is "an inner urge to venture and devote oneself in working in a first-hand kind of way"(Emmet, 1958).

7. Duty undertaken with sober enthusiasm (Schweitzer, in Emmet, 1958).

8. Vocation involves such qualities as perseverance, courage, and imagination (Hansen, 1995).

9. Personal mission that includes individual inheritance, community commitment, and moral intention (Lesage, 1966).

10. Not just holding on. "The commitment holds you. You can't not do the work" (Daloz, Keen, Keen, and Parks, 1996).

When examining the above explanations of vocation, we find several dimensions of the term emerging. First, vocation seems to involve both commitment to others and personal fulfillment. This is best exemplified by Buechner's thoughts on vocation as "where your deep gladness and the world's greatest hunger meet."[10] According to Hansen, vocation is not about selfless devotion. Vocation implies work that is both meaningful and fulfilling.

Second, vocation is characterized as a journey. The journey seems to be about developing oneself over time and involves venturing inside oneself as well as venturing out into the complex world. Sharon Parks has emphasized the value of both "venturing and abiding." She proposed that in order for personal and social transformations to occur, individuals must both engage in the journey to find out about others, but they must also return home to tell the story and validate the experiences, and they must also have a capacity to "stay." The notion of "venturing and abiding" reveals that vocation has both internal and external dimensions.[11]

Third, there is no blueprint for a vocation. We all bring our own natural inheritances to formation of a vocation. According to Lesage, "a vocation embraces talents, individual work, and action in a perfect physical and spiritual fulfillment. It is the building through temperament, attitudes, and aptitudes of a unique human type...."[12] Vocations are carried out by individuals in an active, creative, engaging, imaginative, highly individualistic sort of way. For this reason, Emmet proposes that vocations are not easily interchangeable, and those who fulfill vocations usually have done so in a unique and personal sort of way.[13] Hansen states that individuals working out of a sense of vocation seem to "inhabit their roles," and they put a "personal stamp" on their work.[14]

Fourth, appreciating the details of the work appears to be an important part of enacting a vocation. Hansen's study of teachers' testimonies found evidence of the reality of Smith's notion that enacting a vocation involves "the love of the drudgery it involves."[15] Fine-tuned attention to the details of work does not seem to distract from the work; rather, cultivating an appreciation for the mundane seems to provide a strong base from which to enact a vocation.

Fifth, uncertainty and doubt appear to accompany vocational enactment. Because we often journey forward in response to calls from others, we sometimes find ourselves in places where we may not have full understanding of how we might help, what skills we might need, if we are really making a difference, or if we are the person who is really needed to do the job. Introspection, faith, and courage are often called upon by individuals who find themselves trying to come to terms with the uncertain dimensions of vocation.

Gleanings and adaptations of John Schuster's work, *Answering Your Call*, should serve to further our understanding of the many dimensions of vocation.

- Calls, also known as vocations, are invitations to activate your will toward a cause worthy of you and the human family. They are purpose with a voice; visions turned into commands.

- Calls, or vocations, are part intellectual and part emotional, part human and part divine. A call is sometimes heard as an inner voice, sometimes seen as a mental image, sometimes felt as a push from behind, and sometimes experienced as the voice of God above. A call urges you to go past the surface level and do something that has lasting value.

- No one knows for sure what calls or vocations are. That is the best part about them. Calls and vocations remain in the realm of the mysterious. Calls and vocations have attracted a lot of attention as people try to define them. Most are mistaken. If you know of someone who has a precise or scientific definition, or a poetic or religious definition, and you like it, use it. But don't pretend you know completely what a call is, any more than you know completely what grace is, or what love is. It is more useful not to confine discussions about what calls and vocations are, but to ask what they do.

- Calls and vocations do many things. They provide soul mandates, orders to live the large part of our lives. They cause us to attach ourselves to a cause that pulls us out of the limits of our personal history. Vocational calls draw us to a deeper level of that to which we are currently committed.

- Vocational calls turn companions into lifelong friends, salesmen into service providers, grocery store clerks into health consultants, doctors into healers, secretaries into stewards, bureaucrats into civil servants, writers into storytellers, teachers into dream-makers, parents into mentors, and spouses into soulmates.

- Calls and vocations inspire. They bring and pull out spiritual sensitivities, energy, and insights far more than professional ones.

- Because vocational calls come from a different place and a different time than ours, we need to be quiet long enough and often enough to hear them.

- Carrying out a role because you like it is not responding to a call. A role only becomes a vocation when you will spiritual substance into it. A role becomes a vocation when a person, from within that role, fulfills a need to confront the questions of destiny, isolation, meaning, death, relationships, and spirituality.

- A calling doesn't depend on how big the role is, but how much love we put into it. Do what is small with love, and love will make it count.

- Answering a vocational call will bring mentors into your life. It will also bring tormentors. Often we are our greatest vocational saboteur. Since our egos are never going to go away, we must learn how to skillfully combat our egos. Left unchecked, our egos will muffle or distort the shy whisper of the soul within and the voice of God above—both of which call us past the shallow life and into the joys of a vocational one.[16]

Three Vocational Calls: The Call of Work, the Call of Relationships, and the Call of Faith

Most of us, including those who have authored recent writings on vocation, seem to focus on vocational calls as related primarily to occupation. But it seems far more helpful to understand that vocational callings are found in three key areas of our lives: work, relationships, and faith.

These three vocational calls are often intertwined. Sometimes our vocational journey takes us to places where these three calls are all working together. Sometimes we find ourselves in places where one call may be in tension with another. And sometimes on the vocational journey we find that one call seems to be written in a capital "C," beckoning us to give it far more attention than the other two, which for a time may seem to be written in a lower case "c."

Responding to any of these vocational callings is transformative and reflects a spiritual pursuit. The vocational journey is a spiritual one because it is all about your life, but still not about a life that is all yours. It is about the desire to make the you that is a private individual meaningfully interface with the public.

The difference between those embracing a vocational spirituality and those who do not is like the difference between those deciding to embark on a journey and those deciding to stay in the neighborhood. It is a spiritual journey that enables us to make meaning of the ordinary and sense the sacredness of it. Vocational spirituality becomes accustomed to mystery while never really becoming totally comfortable with it. In describing the spiritual nature of vocations, J. Loder writes:

> Essential to the spirit's nature is its wind-like quality; it often takes us by surprise and leads us where we would not otherwise go. Its deeper characteristic, however is its integrity in driving toward meaning and wholeness in every complex and variegated context.[17]

Here in Part 1, we will look at each of the three vocational callings, as well as the dynamic of discerning those calls. In Part 2, we will make note of the key elements to sustaining the commitments entailed in our three vocational callings. Part 3 identifies challenges putting our vocational lives at risk and offers specific practices that respond to these challenges.

The Call of Work

Traditionally, work was considered a vocation only when we identified the call of work with the call of faith. It had both a sense of calling and a noble sense of service to it. But that does not have to be so.

The call of work addresses the question, "What do I want to do with my life?" and invites us to labor in the area of business, transportation, education, art, entertainment, science, technology, ministry, industrial support, medicine, government, and social services. We would do well to see that the vocational call of work must be done with integrity and guided by ethical principles, but it does not have to be a form of ministry. It does not have to be benevolent or charitable. It does not have to be about serving others.

In order for the call of work to be part of one's vocation and not simply one's career, however, it must evoke spiritual sensitivities within us *and* require spiritual sensitivities from us.

The call of work is vocational when we find that the labor itself satisfies our spirit in ways that may often be beyond words and lends itself to our bringing our spirit forth into the work itself. So graphic designers, marketing professionals, grocery clerks, furniture sales staff, broadcasters, librarians, computer technicians, florists, telephone operators, nurses, bricklayers, mail carriers, engineers, upholsterers, jewelers, antique dealers, and so on may very well be experiencing the vocational call to work, and find that this calling both nourishes their spirituality and allows them natural ways to bring their spirituality into it.

When work provides a means for the inner self to find expression in an outside role, a deep spiritual sense of fulfillment is present.

JUSTWORK

How can work reflect our existing spiritual sensitivities and also cultivate spiritual growth? Perhaps through a three-dimensional dance we have come to call JUSTWORK.

JUSTWORK enables us to more fully enjoy the spiritual nature of the vocational call of work by intentionally honoring and maintaining three distinct aspects of employment. It can be considered a spiritual discipline for the workplace. It is a practice that requires clarity and courage, a little clutch and a little gas. Most of all, JUSTWORK enables us to integrate the values found in the call of faith and the call of relationships.

JUSTwork is that dimension that requires us to maintain the *just* aspects of employment. Here we are asked to do our part in making integrity and honesty the operative values of the work culture. We may be invited to recognize that busy seasons of work should be followed by a brief but slower season that allows us to recoup, refresh, and re-create. This dimension of work may require that we contribute to a culture of trust wherein co-workers are viewed as innately moral and given the benefit of the doubt. It may call us to practice a hermeneutic of generosity instead of a hermeneutic of suspicion.

JUSTwork is also that dimension which respects the currency of meaning. Some workers find this as valuable as money. It asks us to respect the fact that some co-workers need the workplace to be a conversational community wherein people discuss challenges they may be facing in finding meaning or in making sense of other areas of their lives—like relationships, personal growth, or professional expertise. This dimension may ask us to support policies that respect family leave for either gender, or a couple of paid days for community service. Simply put, this is the dimension that asks us to do our part in seeing that work is just.

JustWORK, on the other hand, is that dimension which upholds and respects the fact that employment is by its very nature work. This is the dimension that calls us to embrace high standards of excellence along with authentic affirmation and well-deserved recognition. This is the dimension that asks us to hold ourselves—and allow others to hold us—accountable for the quality of our work. It requires us to understand that, despite the current infatuation we all have about leadership, workmanship is more valuable than leadership.

JustWORK reflects an ethic of productivity and service which may have to take precedence over an ethic of process and dialogue. It invites us to embrace tough questions about performance and evaluation. At its best, this dimension invites us to do productive work creatively by recognizing that specific projects and tasks can be done by specific people regardless of their job title or rank of command. It invites us to see that good, productive, successful work can be done when we see how co-workers are smart instead of how smart co-workers are.

At its core, this dimension of workplace spirituality asks us to honor and embrace the fact that work is *work*.

Just work is the third dimension. **Just work** refrains from capitalizing any aspect of work. Instead, this is the dimension that fiercely attempts to reclaim some of the other aspects of life that we have given up, neglected, or abused for the sake of work.

Just work is the dimension which maintains that, within the bigger social system of our lives, work is not our primary community. Primary support, self-actualization, relationships, faith, and personal growth does not have to be an expectation of the workplace. Instead, the social system and subsystem of family, friends, and neighbors, civic and recreational groups, congregations and faith communities, holidays and holy days, kitchens and commons remain the fertile ground of primary communities.

In this dimension, there are no covert or overt expectations regarding relationship-building within the culture of the workplace. Each person is encouraged to work cooperatively, effectively, and generously with others, but each person is encouraged to draw their personal support from significant others outside the workplace. Workers can certainly develop strong and even life-giving relationships with co-workers, but the culture of the workplace shouldn't make anyone feel obligated to do so.

Just work does not place on work unrealistically high expectations for happiness. This is the dimension of a workplace spirituality that never loses sight of the bigger sources of grace and fulfillment. Compared to faith, life, and love, work is *just work*.

And so we see that when we can respond to the call of work with a spirituality similar to **JUSTWORK** we engage in a creative struggle for balance. Sometimes we stress the conviction that work should be just, other times we embrace the demands that work should be effective and hard, and through it all, we are asked to keep work in perspective given the other callings of our lives. It is a workplace spirituality that integrates the heart of the call of faith and the call of relationships.

The Call of Relationships

The call of relationships addresses the question "Who will I be with?" and invites us to respond to those we choose to travel with on life's journey. The call of relationships is the "call of we" and contains the joys and responsibilities of traveling life's journey with family members, as spouses, siblings, parents, single, ordained, or members of religious communities. The following conversation exemplifies what we have come to understand as the call of relationships:

A private investigator for a public defender's office who had served in Vietnam in his youth and later went on to get a masters degree in history was now committed to helping poor people get a fair chance at justice. After an hour of talking about his work, he was asked if he considered his work to be a vocation. "You mean, like a spiritual thing?"

When the person posing the vocational question shrugged, the private investigator continued: "It's a good fit. And I do it well. But the thing is that it allows my wife to keep her job as the head of nursing at the hospital. She's great at it and she deserves it. Plus my two daughters get to stay in their high school without moving. You see, we live about two hours from here. I stay in a little apartment on Monday and Tuesday. Then I drive home Wednesday and come back for Thursday and Friday. I'm back home Friday after work and we all have the weekends together. And then there are always three-day weekends like the one coming up."

The private investigator never directly answered whether or not he considered his noble work to be a vocation. He didn't have to. His response clearly indicated that the call of relationships was his real calling at this time. He had chosen work which best allowed him to respond to the needs of his family.

Many of us give the call of relationships priority over the call of work. Recently, the *New York Times* magazine ran a cover feature on the many high-powered women choosing to "head home" instead of heading corporations.

The scene in this cozy Atlanta living room would, at first glance, warm an early feminist's heart the eight women in this room have each earned a degree from Princeton. And after Princeton, the women of this book club went on to do things that women were not expected to do. They received law degrees from Harvard and Columbia. They chose husbands who could keep up with them, not simply support them. They waited to have children because work was too exciting. They put on power suits and marched off to take on the world.[18]

Imagine interviewing these women in the midst of their "exciting work," taking on the world and using the knowledge and skills they had honed. Imagine asking them, in the midst of this time in their lives, if they considered their work to be their vocation. Chances are many of these eight women would have responded with some affirmation that this work did reflect a calling. Some would probably say that they were feeling fulfilled, that the roles they had carved out were compatible with their inner strengths and natural tendencies. Some would even articulate spiritual sensitivities to explain the happiness and gratitude they were experiencing in their work.

But that would have been then—not now. The women in the Atlanta living room have responded to another calling:

> "I don't want to be on the fast track leading to a partnership at a prestigious law firm....Some people define that as success. I don't," says Katherine Brokaw, who left that track in order to stay home with her three children. Another member of the group, Sally Sears, had been a highly successful news reporter. At first she wanted to be "a confirmed single person, childless, a world traveler. I would have hung in there, except the days kept getting longer and longer....My five-day, fifty-hour week was becoming a sixty-hour week....My son, Will, was growing up, and I was driving home from a fire...I knew there would always be wrecks and fires, but there wouldn't always be his childhood."

Another member of the group, Vicky McElhaney Benedict, decided to quit her job at Emory University and head home after giving birth to her first child. She had a second child three years later. Benedict states:

> "This is what I was meant to do," she says. "I hate to say that because it sounds like I should have skipped college. But I mean this is what I was meant to do at this time. I know that's very un-p.c. [politically correct], but I like life's rhythms when I'm nurturing a child."

A survey by the research firm Catalyst revealed that twenty-six percent of women at the cusp of the highest level of management don't want the promotion. *Fortune* magazine found that of the 108 women listed among their top fifty most powerful, twenty have chosen to leave their high powered jobs for lives less intense and more fulfilling.

But the call of relationships is not simply heard by working women giving up careers in order to head home. People do this all the time. We give our hearts to relationships, be it with a spouse, a sibling, a child, a community, a church, a parent, or a friend. We sustain both the commitment and the love. You see, the characteristic that distinguishes the call of relationships from the other two vocational callings is *love*.

Consider the following news article. The headline read "Closer Sasaki Decides Not To Pitch For Mariners In 2004," but the opening sentence presented the call of relationships:

> Kazuhiro Sasaki has decided to leave the Seattle Mariners to stay home in Japan with his family. In his first year here in America he was voted baseball's Rookie of the Year. In his second year, the fans of America voted him on to the American League's All-Star team. In just four years he saved 129 games, a Mariner team record. His agent explained, "It's a personal situation. He wanted to stay home with his kids. Last year he did not have his kids with him or his wife. He had to have that, and he left a lot of money on the table."[19]

Kazuhiro Sasaki gave up $9.5 million in order to answer the call of relationships.

Consciously and unconsciously, intentionally and spontaneously, we respond to the call of relationships in a series of decisions to renew the commitment and the love. It can be described as the kind of renewal process "to repeat a promise made," and to "restore and reestablish, take up again, resume."[20]

Alone and together, responding to the call of relationship is about cultivating knowledge of another: intimate, often budding knowledge of another's dreams, fears, past, potential, passions, and personhood. This "coming to know" another requires that we demonstrate a presence that is both tender and strong. It requires each of us to remain actively present to another's becoming.

Unlike the two other vocational callings, responding to the call of relationships takes place within a constant state of vulnerability and grace. Researcher Sharon Parks reminds us that in the call of relationships is a call to love tenderly with informed sensitivity as presented in the Hebrew Scriptures:

> To love tenderly is to love with an awareness of the capacity of the other to be wounded, to suffer pain, and to be dependent upon relationship with others. To love tenderly requires a particular capacity and informed sensitivity.[21]

The call of relationships is the messy one. Maintaining our response to this call requires a fierce holding onto the voices of human desire. It requires a strong effort to recognize and embrace, not transcend, the weaknesses and fragilities of others. It is the human embracing of another's humanity. It is this acceptance of another in order to focus on the essential needs of those with whom we choose to maintain relationships.

The call of relationships lacks the solitary nature of the call of faith. It lacks the serenity found in the various practices of faith such as prayer and meditation. Instead, the call of relationship features the ups and downs of another's life, one's own emotional needs, and the intensity of expectations associated with love. Parks points out that "we are called not only to be tender, but also to be intensely determined to hold firm to life."[22]

But the call of relationships is not restricted to committing just to another person. It can also be a call to commit to a relationship with a movement, an organization, a school of thought. We can feel called to establish a deep and abiding relationship with an environmental program, a political party, a community service agency, a charity, a mental health program like Alcoholics Anonymous, or a social ideology.

Responding to the call of relationships by relating to a group or movement can indeed bring us a richer experience of life and at the same time call us into life-giving dynamics of self-sacrifice and commitment to the well-being of others. But this kind of relating has two built-in dangers.

Relating to a group, movement, program, school of thought, or organization cannot be a substitute for authentic and strong relationships with another human. When this occurs, a soulful side of ourselves atrophies like an unused muscle. We cannot experience the soulful "coming to know" another when relating to a program or ideology replaces our interpersonal relationships. We cannot share in the intimate and sacred journey of another person's process of becoming if we choose to relate to agencies or political movements *instead* of individuals.

The second danger of a deep and committed relating to groups, movements, organizations, or causes is a tendency to make others into enemies. Even though we are usually "called" by the good work being pursued by such groups and programs, the passionate pursuit of making a difference too often fuels itself on an "ethic of the enemy."[23] In our passionate relationships with groups or programs making a difference, we can easily establish someone else as the cause of the problem. We easily decide that another person or group must be defeated, abolished, or overcome. Note now the irony and the paradox in this dynamic: we respond (soulfully) to the call of relationships by diminishing relationships with those who oppose us.

The spiritual richness in living out a committed relationship with a group, organization, movement, or program can be best harvested when we consciously do the good and noble work of helping others without deliberately casting others as obstacles or destructive forces. It is about holding the contradictions and paradox of imperfection or differences as we seek to contribute to the common good.

In summary, the call of relationship involves coming to know another, choosing to love another, cultivating tenderness and strength, while tenaciously holding on to life. The call of relationships involves responding more completely to the voices of human desire, vulnerability, strength, and knowledge.

Despite the high-maintenance nature of the call of relationship, it is the one vocational call that brings us the most experiences of life. While the call of faith can keep us grounded in right relationship with God and with the children of God, as well as bring us inner peace, it is through the call of relationships that we can actually taste the fresh fruit of a loving act. In the highly charged environs of the call of relationships we can feel the strength of another's support, laugh at what is humorous, marvel at the beauty in children, find security in the touch of loved ones, and play an intimate, sacred role in being part of another human's becoming.

Here, in the call of relationships, we experience love in the most human ways. We live out our natural tendency to be social beings and spiritual ones. Here, we integrate our natural instincts to care for self by committing to others. Here, we choose to take the path of life characterized by sharing instead of the path characterized by solitary navigation. It is the call of "we," not just "me."

The spiritual tasks in responding to the call of relationships have to do with balance.

- How are we to balance the giving of ourselves without having another take advantage of our giving?
- How do we balance our interest with the interest of those we choose to be with? How do we balance consoling with confronting, listening with advising?
- How do we forgive a cruel act without endorsing it?
- How do we voice our needs without imposing them?

- How do we let others "come to know" us without fully revealing that which we want to keep to ourselves?

- How do we take relational risks without being irresponsible?

- How do we love well and true?

- How are we to exercise and balance our call to relationships at work?

- Is it ever important to give the call of relationships more attention than the call of faith?

- Is it ever best to reconsider the responses we have been making to the call of relationships, in view of the new insights and growth we may be experiencing?

When asked "Do you believe in God?", ninety-four to ninety-five percent of Americans respond, "Yes." (Roof)[24]

More than four in five Americans say they have "experienced God's presence or a spiritual force" close to them, and forty-six percent report that it has happened many times. "People are reaching out in all directions in their attempt to escape from the seen world to the unseen world. There is a deep desire for spiritual moorings—a hunger for God," explains pollster George Gallup, Jr. More than three in four Americans believe all religions have at least some elements of truth. Nearly seventy percent of Americans' spiritual experiences are the most important part of religion. Seventy percent of Christians in the United States say they should be tolerant of people of another faith, and only twenty-four percent think it's their duty to convert members of another faith. (Shaler)[25]

Fifty-three percent of Americans prefer to pray alone and meditate, while twenty-nine percent prefer to worship with others. (Roof)[26]

The Call of Faith

The call of faith is both our most basic and our highest calling. It addresses the question "How am I to live my life?" and invites the same response for all people, whether Christian, Jew, Muslim, Hindu: "As a child of God."

Responding to the call of faith is a three-dimensional response that invites us to attend to the religious (vertical), the moral (horizontal), and the inner personal (internal) dimensions of our lives.

The *vertical dimension* of the call of faith invites each of us to invest in and maintain a personal relationship with the Creator. Within or outside of religious traditions, our vertical responses to the call of faith usually takes the form of prayer, submission, and openness to the transcendent, as well as various forms of inquiry and study.

The vertical dimension of the call of faith invites all of us to look at our experiences with religious imagination. Sharon Parks points out that when it comes time to describe the process of making meaning of our lives, which is both the most ultimate and intimate aspect of our consciousness, we reserve the word "faith." According to Parks,

> Meaning and faith are composed by means of the imagination....It is by means of images, metaphors, and symbols that we shape into one the chaos of our existence, that we simplify and unify, that we apprehend, though we can never comprehend—the real. It is by means of disciplined imagination that we search out fitting and right images by which to apprehend truth and compose the meanings we shall live by.[27]

In researching the spiritual journeys of Baby Boomers, Wade Roof discovered:

> The whole question of religious imagination, or how the divine gets pictured symbolically, is enormously important, and touches upon the more subtle spiritual changes now underway among Boomers.[28]

Responding to vocational callings is more about the exercise of a spirituality than a theology. Theology brings us the insight, beauty, truth, wisdom, and discipline of careful thought about the seen and unseen. Theology *explains*. It seeks ways of understanding. Spirituality *lives*. It seeks ways of being.

When it comes to our understanding and experience of vocation, applying theological perspectives, tenets, and traditions do not do it justice. The noted theologian Bernard Cooke reminds us that people of all religions respond to the call of faith with

> a set of principles, insights, and critical judgments that equips us to interpret our experiences in a more accurate and profound way. Religiously, the manner in which each of us interprets his or her experiences is the springboard for thinking about the divine. Much of the interpretation of what happens around us does not come through clear understandings we already have. Rather, it comes at a level of an emotional response, our "gut reactions."[29]

Responding to the call of faith is largely a matter of honoring our religious imagination. Through the exercise of our religious imagination we experience moments in which we sense the sacred. According to James Roy King those moments include:

1. *"Aha" moments* of enlightenment, discovery, insight, or wisdom. Such moments have been described by people of all faith traditions, including Buddhists who refer to these moments as satori.

2. *Moments of confrontation* which bring an intense critique of one's behaviors, attitudes, or assumptions.

3. *Historical or eventful moments* that mark a significant decision or growth in one's spiritual life. Our imagination allows us to mark such moments private, informal ways or communal, formal ways, i.e., a bar mitzvah, baptism, vow, commitment rite, altar call, and so on.

4. *Moments of grace* in which we experience a sense of protection, strength, blessing, or assistance directly from God above or through the Spirit in others.

5. *Moments related to place* where we literally experience the sacred in the form of truth, beauty, or love. Such places can be our own personal and private windows to the sacred, like a certain inner city tenement window, country lane, wooded park, ocean beach, childhood playground, or rooftop vista. But religious imagination also enables places to be formally honored and esteemed by mainline religious traditions, i.e., Muslim Mecca, the Judaic Wailing Wall, the Christian Holy Land of the New Testament.[30]

Responding to vocational callings is less about cognitive understanding and more about emotional longings and soulful desires. In 1758, philosopher Jean-Jacques Rousseau wrote to a young Emile in what we might now consider vocational advice:

> It is one of the faults of our age to rely too much on cold reason. As if men [humans] were all mind....In our attempt to appeal to reason only, we have reduced our precepts to words: we have not embodied them in deed. Mere reason is not active: occasionally she restrains, more rarely she stimulates, but she never does a great thing. Small minds have a mania for reasoning. Strong souls speak a very different language, and it is by this language that men [all of us] are persuaded and driven to action.[31]

The religions of the world have come to ritualize this call of faith and our response to it with practices, various rites of passage and commitment, and holy seasons of prayer and/or fasting. For many of us, religious rituals, practices, and traditions hold great meaning and power as responses to the vocational call of faith. But we also know that an increasing amount of people respond to the call of faith outside of religious affiliations. Research tells us that spiritual interests among Americans, for example, is reaching an all-time high, while membership in mainline religions has declined.[32]

Responding to the call of faith is far more than developing a personal relationship with the Creator. The *horizontal dimension* of this call invites us to contribute to the well-being of the rest of the Creator's children or the earth. This is the human dimension of the call of faith. At the heart of the call of faith's moral dimension is the conviction that we are all related. The moral, or horizontal, dimension of the call of faith invites us to live a loving life in which we invest in the well-being of others. Traditionally, our horizontal response to the call of faith is found in the practice of virtues.

The moral dimension to the call of faith holds us accountable. It is not enough to pray regularly while ignoring the chance to help those in need. It is not enough to attend Sunday service and tell racist jokes on Wednesday. It is not enough to wear a religious medal around your neck and shoot rival gang members. It is not enough to pray five times a day and commit acts of terrorism.

The third dimension of our response to the call to faith invites us to develop the awareness of the essence and soulful nature of ourselves. This third response, or *internal dimension*, to the call of faith invites us to tap into the spiritual resources that enable us to recognize our internal inheritances, seek ways to use these gifts, acknowledge our shadows, overcome our fears, recognize moments of grace, reach our potential, stay hopeful in the face of despair, move through grief, get up after failure, and accept our own shortcomings. In short, internal responses to the call of faith aim at helping us to know exactly who we are while dreaming to be more than we are.

Vocationally, the internal dimension of the call of faith does not invite us to handle emotions of our daily lives so that we don't freak out when we can't find the remote, stress out over waxy build-up on our floors, misplace our reading glasses, forget cell phone numbers, or fall off our diets. The value of developing a healthy internal dimension of our spirituality is so that we can deal with our own inconsistencies, contradictions, compulsions, and conflicts.

Vocationally speaking, the internal dimension of the call to faith helps us overcome our internal noise so that we can better hear our soulful desires. In this way, the internal dimension of our spirituality helps us better know our authentic self. According to Parker Palmer, when the our true nature is enacted in our work it is an "alignment of the role and the soul."[33]

All three dimensions of the call of faith are distinct and overlapping, like three interlocking circles. Sometimes a vertical response to the call of faith—like attending a worship service or a private prayerful meditation—can help you stop obsessing over a personal flaw (internal). Sometimes a horizontal response, like reaching out to another in need, may have a positive effect on the vertical dimension of your spirituality by reawakening in you a sense of gratitude to God for your own good fortune.

The challenge of responding to the call of faith lies in attending to all three dimensions of the call. Each of us, at different times in our lives, may find that one dimension of the call of faith is more dominant than the others. For a season, we may enjoy a spirituality that makes it easy to lead the loving life (horizontal), but we may feel out of touch with the Creator (vertical). Other times we may find ourselves enjoying a certain private and prayerful connection with the sacred (vertical) while remaining in an oppositional relationship with a spouse, sibling, colleague, or neighbor (horizontal). Sometimes we may find ourselves freely and willingly living out loving commitments to others (horizontal) while being unable to overcome pains, anxieties, or confusions (internal).

The call of faith addresses the question, "how am I to live?" By answering "as a child of God," we are invited to take stock of the religious, moral, and emotional state of our lives, intentionally addressing the least developed dimension(s). The courageous self-examination of these three dimensions represents the transformative power of answering the call of faith, and clarifies the reason it is our most basic and important vocational calling.

We do not need to respond alone. Our responses to the three dimensions of the call of faith can be made with the help of friends, family members, loved ones, communities, and groups.

Discerning the Calls

After September 11, 2001, an All-Pro football player for the Arizona Cardinals approached his coach. "We have to talk," he said. Pat Tillman went on to tell his coach that he had decided to walk away from his successful football career in order to join the Army. He refused all requests for interviews and privately joined the Rangers for a three-year stint in the Middle East. Two years later, ESPN awarded he and his brother Kevin the Arthur Ashe Courage Award. A short time later, Pat Tillman was killed in combat while on patrol in Afghanistan. Upon hearing the news, Coach Dave McGinnis made this statement: "Pat knew his purpose in life. He proudly walked away from a career in football to a greater calling."[34]

Vocational spirituality is a journey of becoming. It is about developing oneself over time, and it involves venturing inside oneself and venturing out into the complex world. Enactment of vocational spirituality involves venturing out into the unknown areas of faith, relationships, and work with a willingness to explore the callings there. It is a journey of transformation as we increase our discoveries about the self, the sacred, and the social by responding with commitments.

Sharon Parks emphasizes the value of both "venturing and abiding" in order to experience the transformative effect of vocational sensitivities and commitments. We must both engage in the journey of discovery and return home to tell the stories and validate the experiences. We must also have the capacity to "stay" instead of just passing through.[35]

Discerning vocational callings is like dancing the two-step. Step one involves determining where the call is coming from. Step two involves discovering which call you are responding to.

Step one

Vocation comes from the root word for "the call." No debate. But where do you imagine the call is coming from? If you imagine that it is coming from the voice of God somewhere outside of you, you will spend your time trying to get in touch with the transcendent. But if you are not careful, you may never discern the degree to which the voice from "outside" is compatible with who you are within.

Referring to teachers, Parker Palmer writes: "Any authentic call ultimately comes from the voice of the teacher within, the voice that invites me to honor the true nature of my self."[36] The voice of the friend within is from the same family as the voice that is beyond us. To not see the related and holy nature of the two is a mistake.

> In popular conception, theism involves the notion of a God up there or out there somewhere, and thus distant and removed from life in this world. One problem with this image of humanity's relationship with the divine, as Matthew Fox points out, is that it stifles the soul. He notes, as Jung warned, the one way to kill the soul is to "worship a God outside you."[37]

On the other hand, by listening only to our inner voice we may miss out on the challenges that can come from the listening to and submitting to the voice of God who is beyond us.

Step two

Which call are you discerning, the call of faith, the call of relationships, or the call of work? Vocational spirituality consists of distinguishing between each of them while also being sensitive to the ways they are interconnected.

Traditionally, we have limited ourselves to discerning some kind of all-purpose call usually related to work. Vocational spirituality involves asking ourselves how a certain call of work may enhance or hinder the commitments, responsibilities, and opportunities present in the way you are living out the call of relationships. Likewise, it is a spirituality that involves asking ourselves how a certain call of relationships will enhance or hinder the commitments, responsibilities, and opportunities present in the way you are living out the call of faith.

It makes most sense to always start the discerning process by asking these four questions:

1. Where is the call coming from?
2. Which of the three vocational calls is it?
3. How will my response to this call affect the way I live out the other two calls?
4. What role is this call asking me to take, and to what degree does the role align with my soul?

Whether the call you are discerning is coming primarily from the friend within your soulful self, the voices of human desire, or straight from the voice of God beyond us, Schuster says we will always find at least four obstacles to responding:

1. The noise of life, which consists of the tasks, stresses, and chaos that drown out the voice that calls. The noise of life can be so loud that we simply can't hear the voice that calls.
2. Other voices come from all kinds of sources: friends and family, mentors and tormentors, events and coincidences, phone calls and favorite songs. Other voices are an obstacle when any one of them has us listening to the wrong source(s).
3. Call avoidance is an obstacle when we hear the voice issuing the call but try not to answer it. Oftentimes we practice call avoidance when we operate out of fear, complacency, or fatigue.

4. The doldrums represent those times when the wind of the Spirit is simply not blowing. Your vocational journey is adrift without any direction or energy. It is a time of dead silence. No voice is calling. This is a natural time that comes out of nowhere. Like the real doldrums on the sea, you didn't bring this period of inertia upon your self, nor can you really do anything to jump start it again. Please don't accept the sailors' doldrums superstition that someone is bad luck and throw that person overboard. Vocational spirituality, after all, embraces mystery. All you can do in the doldrums is wait it out and keep drinking enough fluids to stay healthy.[38]

Discerning the call is essentially a spiritual practice of prayer or meditation. Through a variety of prayer forms and settings, it is a commitment to exercise our "ears to hear and eyes to see." It's about curiosity, courage, and the unfolding of belief and trust. Vocational calls are not cognitive ones; they are soulful ones. Regardless of whether they represent something in the call of faith, call of relationships, or call of work, vocational calls stir the spirit.

If a call does not spark your passion, it probably isn't a vocational one. If a call does not evoke and require an enduring commitment from you, it is probably not a vocational one.

There are imitations of the three vocational calls:

- If the call of work does not resonate with your natural talents and interests, it may be a call to revenue. It may offer you employment but not fulfillment.

- If the call of relationship does not propel you to enduring love, it may be a call to social and interpersonal interactions. It will allow you to survive on social skills instead of intimacy.

- If the call of faith is not compelling you to live as a child of God, it may be a call to religious membership or spiritual convenience. It will allow you to take a tour instead of making a pilgrimage.

Like all good prayer forms, discerning a call is characterized by humble listening, curiosity, courageous honesty, and authentic gratitude. These virtues show up in the prayerful and sensitive conversations we have over coffee with a friend, the solitary reflections we conduct with ourselves, the inventories we take of our light and our shadows, our fears and our dreams, our commitments and our compulsions, our past and our present, our ancestors and our children, our goodbyes and our hellos.

We can practice prayerful discernment through our headphones, sitting in the bleachers at a ball game, in our favorite chair after the kids go to bed, or in our churches, synagogues, temples, and mosques. We can exercise our "ears to hear and eyes to see" and cultivate our spiritual sensitivities driving home from work, puttering in a garden, sitting in a crowded restaurant, or browsing in the bookstore.

Because vocational callings ask us to assess the compatibility between a role and our soul, we must rely on practices that consist of a certain kind of humble listening, curiosity, courageous honesty, and authentic gratitude. Paper and pencil surveys, personality assessments, and psychological profiles have a place in our lives. But they aren't suitable for the kind of discernment process that cultivates the spiritual sensitivities needed to exercise our "ears to hear and eyes to see."

Vocational spirituality is characterized by a consistent openness and examination of the movements within each of the three calls. It is the integration of your internal beliefs and your external experiences. Vocational spirituality is not characterized by a developmental, sequential, and predicable unfolding of growth. Vocational spirituality respects mystery enough not to try and control it. It requires that we develop spiritual sensitivities in addition to professional ones.

For Reflection

1. To which of the three vocational calls—work, relationships, or faith—are you attending to the most these days? How and when did you first hear each of these calls? Which call(s) might you be neglecting?

2. Which dimension of JUSTWORK is dominant in your life right now?

_____ JUSTwork
_____ JustWORK
_____ just work

Which one are you being most called to address right now?

3. Within your response to the call of relationships, which questions of balance (listed on pages 23-24) do you need to address?

4. Which dimension of your response to the call of faith is your strongest?

_____ the vertical
_____ the horizontal
_____ the internal

Which one(s) do you need to further develop?

5. Which of these obstacles to discerning your call hinder you most?

_____ the noise of life
_____ other voices
_____ call avoidance
_____ the doldrums

6. What vocational task(s) now await you?

Endnotes

1. Allen, James. *As a Man Thinketh*. Philadelphia: Running Press, 2001.

2. Der-Hovanessian, Diana. *Selected Poems*. Riverdale-on Hudson, NY: Sheep Meadow Press, 1997.

3. Serow, R. "Called to Teach: A Study of Highly Motivated Preservice Teachers." *Journal of Research and Development in Education*, 27 (1994), 65-72.

4. Frankena, W. "The Philosophy of Thought." *Thought*, 51 (1976), 393-404.

5. Emmet, Dorothy Mary. *Function, Purpose, and Powers: Some Concepts in the Study of Individuals and Societies*. London: Macmillan, 1958.

6. Serow, "Called to Teach," 65-72.

7. Hansen, David. *The Call to Teach*. New York: The Teacher's College Press, 1995.

8. Hacking, Ian. *The Social Construction of What?* Cambridge, MA: Harvard University Press, 1999.

9. The following selections come from the following sources:

   1. and 2. Hansen, *The Call to Teach*.

   3. Smith, Logan. *All Trivia: Trivia, More Trivia, Afterthoughts, Last Words*. New York: Harcourt, Brace and Company, 1945.

   4. Buechner, Frederick. *Wishful Thinking: A Seeker's ABC*. San Francisco: HarperSanFrancisco, 1993.

   5. Palmer, Parker. *The Courage to Teach: Exploring the Inner Landscape of a Teacher's Life*. San Francisco: Jossey-Bass, 1998.

   6. Emmet, *Function, Purpose, and Powers*.

   7. Schweitzer, in Emmet above.

   8. Hansen, *The Call to Teach*.

   9. Lesage, Germain. *Personalism and Vocation*. Staten Island, NY: Alba House, 1966.

   10. Daloz, Laurent, Cheryl Keen, James Keen, and Sharon Parks. *Common Fire: Leading Lives of Commitment in a Complex World*. Boston: Beacon Press, 1996.

10. Buechner, *Wishful Thinking*.

11. Parks, Sharon. "Home and Pilgrimage: Metaphors for Personal and Social Transformation." *Soundings*, Winter 1989, 298-315.

12. Lesage, *Personalism and Vocation*.

13. Emmet, *Function, Purpose, and Powers*.

14. Hansen, *The Call to Teach*.

15. Ibid.

16. Schuster, John P. *Answering Your Call: A Guide to Living Your Deepest Purpose*. San Francisco: Berrett-Koehler, 2003.

17. Loder, James. *The Transforming Moment*. Colorado Springs, CO: Helmers & Howard, 1989.

18. Belkin, Lisa. "The Opt-Out Revolution." *New York Times Magazine*, October 26, 2003, 42-47.

19. Armstrong, J. Associated Press Sports, January 21, 2004.

20. Bolin, Frances and Judith Falk, eds. *Teacher Renewal: Professional Issues, Personal Choices*. New York: Teachers College Press, 1987.

21. Brueggeman, Walter, et al. *To Act Justly, Love Tenderly, Walk Humbly: An Agenda for Ministers*. New York: Paulist Press, 1986.

22. Ibid.

23. Shriver, D.W. *An Ethic of Enemies: Forgiveness in Politics*. New York: Oxford University Press, 1995.

24. Roof, Wade Clark. *A Generation of Seekers: The Spiritual Journeys of the Baby Boom Generation*. New York: HarperCollins, 1994.

25. Sheler, J. "The Ways of Worship." *U.S. News & World Report*, Mysteries of Faith special edition, 2003, 7-15.

26. Roof, *A Generation of Seekers*.

27. Parks, Sharon. "Social Vision and Moral Courage: Mentoring a New Generation." *Cross Currents*, 40 (1990), 350-67.

28. Roof, *A Generation of Seekers*.

29. Cooke, Bernard. *Sacraments and Sacramentality*. Mystic, CT: Twenty-Third Publications, 1994.

30. King, J. "The Moment as a Theological Category." *Studies in Formative Spirituality*, 9 (1988), 79-95.

31. Jean-Jacques Rousseau. *Emile B. Foxley*, trans. J.M.Dent Publishers, 1974.

32. Roof, *A Generation of Seekers*.

33. Palmer, *The Courage to Teach*.

34. The Associated Press, 2004.
35. Parks, "Home and Pilgrimage."
36. Palmer, *The Courage to Teach.*
37. Roof, *A Generation of Seekers.*
38. Schuster, *Answering Your Call.*

Part 2

Vocational Commitments

*C*herish your vision; cherish your ideals; cherish the music that stirs in your heart, the beauty that forms in your mind, the liveliness that drapes your purest thoughts, for out of them will grow all delightful conditions, all heavenly environments; of these, if you but remain true to them, your world will at last be built.[1]

—James Allen

*S*ustaining the Spirit that fuels the vocational callings of life takes time and rarely happens without struggle. It consists of taking care of the soul and attending to both the spiritual and concrete dimensions of our callings, commitments, and vocational challenges. It consists not only of recognizing the ways things are, but it also involves reclaiming the vision and values that first called to you.

Our thinking on these matters was deeply influenced by the research represented in *Common Fire: Leading Lives of Commitment in a Complex World,* by Laurent Daloz, Cheryl and James Keen, and Sharon Parks.[2] A review of other research and several years of conversations with other people in seminars, on retreat days, and around kitchen tables have led us to believe that there are at least a dozen keys to sustaining the Spirit of vocational commitment.

We hope that exploration of these vocational dynamics will assist you in the ongoing process of examining the three vocational calls of your life and discovering the spiritual dimensions of your vocational commitments.

1. Vocational Seasons

In training facilitators for *The Courage to Teach* program, Parker Palmer suggests that the teaching vocation consists of seasons.[3] The same can be said for each and every vocational response to the call of work, the call of relationships, and the call of faith.

During different times within the call of work, for example, we may be in spring, full of hope, new initiatives, and fresh starts. At other times, we may be in summer, enjoying the warm weather, abundant fruit, a relaxed pace—the season of low maintenance. Some of us are in a winter season of deep introspection, dormancy, and cold weather. Others may be experiencing a fall of harvest, excitement, diversity, or transition. What's more, we may be experiencing a different season within each of the three different vocational calls. The season of our relationships may be different than the season we are experiencing in work or faith.

Palmer's image of vocational seasons is of great help in sustaining the Spirit. If we are in a season we don't enjoy, it doesn't necessarily mean that it's time to change our vocational choices. We can take consolation in knowing that the season will pass. If we live or work with someone who is currently in a wonderful season, we don't have to feel inferior or jealous; we can share that person's good fortune. On the other hand, if we are in a glorious vocational season, we can enjoy it to the full but remember, it is only a season.

No one knows how we get into a certain vocational season, or how we can get out of a certain season. That is as it should be. It is part of the mystery at work in every vocation.

2. Natural Dimensions

Each vocational response has its own natural characteristics and dimensions. Specific feelings, thoughts, and experiences come with specific vocational choices. We are mistaken to think that we can change this.

Within the call of work, for example, educators consistently report that the vocation to teach comes with the conviction that you can succeed despite economic, domestic, or institutional deficits. Yet it also comes with moments of doubt about your effectiveness as a teacher. These are the two natural dimensions of the vocation: confidence that you can successfully overcome deficits and occasional doubt about effectiveness. If you answer the call of work, you will experience both.

The vocation of parenthood has its own natural dimension within the call of relationships. The vocational response of parenting comes with specific joys, anxiety, frustration, hopes, and dreams, as does the vocational response of marriage. Each calling has built-in experiences, emotions, and thoughts that naturally come with the role.

Within the call of faith, denominational membership comes with natural and distinct emotions, dynamics, and thoughts. Different practices of prayer each have their own dynamics and effects. Some, by their very nature, are joyous. Others are more introspective. Communal worship addresses certain needs, while solitary centering prayer has other inherent dimensions.

Some vocational choices are naturally more extroverted than introverted, more physical than sedentary, or more collaborative than self-contained. Don't choose to be a manager if you don't want to interact with people all day. Don't choose to go into sales if you don't want to persuade; don't get married if you don't like partnering. Too many books on vocation perpetuate the misconception that your vocational responses will always be sweet. It is a dangerous myth that can lead us to bail out of our true vocational choices when we experience something bitter or bland, tense or burdensome, frustrating or exhausting.

Accepting the natural dimensions of our different vocational responses goes a long way in helping us sustain the Spirit. Vocationally, it is much more productive to decide how and when you can relieve the natural tension that comes with parenting, alleviate the natural stress that comes with a certain kind of work, enhance the natural dynamics that comes with membership in a faith community, or add a little spice to a vocational role that naturally comes with a bit of drudgery.

Sustaining our vocational commitments includes accepting and even honoring the natural dimensions of each vocational role we choose within work, relationships, and faith.

3. Blessed Assurance

Vocational spirituality can be risky. In it you place yourself and your commitments in plain sight before friends, family, colleagues, God, and everyone in between. Some of us become timid with fear and rarely venture out to fully embrace the possibilities and potential that await those who go forth with confidence about their abilities within the call of work, relationships, and faith.

Most of us know what we are capable of. Most of us believe that we have something worthwhile to contribute. Someplace, somewhere, somehow, we come to trust ourselves enough to venture forth with our desires and abilities. According to the research conducted by Daloz, Keen, Keen, and Parks, a sense of trust and a knowledge of what you are capable of is foundational to sustaining a life of commitment.[4]

This core sense of confidence was given to you by someone else. Someone in your past assured you—*convinced* you—that you were trustworthy and capable of contributing to the good of others. For example, a college professor, in describing his vocational journey, remarked that "In the eyes of my mother, I was always more than I really was."

This sense of trusting yourself and your ability to make a contribution is never learned all at once or once and for all. Given the challenges of responding to the call of work, relationships, and faith, every once in a while you may need to find a way to emotionally revisit someone who was significant in your life to recapture and reclaim the blessed assurance she or he gave you.

4. Engagement with Others

While it is important to be given blessed assurance about yourself, it is just as crucial to experience significant and constructive engagement with others. Doing so enables you to see firsthand the goodness of other people, and to recognize the power of collaboration and community. Constructive engagement with others in matters of faith, relationships, or work can replenish your level of empathy, and remind you that styles and approaches different from your own also bear fruit.[5]

Engagement *with* others also means engagement *for* others. Many people believe that nothing can be truly vocational without contributing toward the well-being of others. While serving others is not the litmus test of one's vocation, the call of work, relationships, or faith is not solely about serving one's self.

Engagement with others is about being part of a good greater than yourself. It requires that you develop a sense of trust in others and what others have to offer. Engagement with others sustains your spirit by pulling you past your own worries and limitations. When you are experiencing an unpleasant vocational season, constructive engagement with others restores your faith in people and renews your belief that good things can be accomplished in each of our callings.

Contrary to some views, vocational spirituality is not a solitary journey. It is true that, ultimately, we should each make vocational choices that best align our roles with our souls. It is through constructive engagement with and for others, however, that we see how our authentic selves, with all their flaws and graces, relate to the larger community.

5. Multiple Belongings

A wealth of resources come to those who have learned to be comfortable among different groups of people. Further, sustaining the Spirit may be easier for those who may have been raised in one core group of people but now have learned how to move smoothly within another group of people of a different economic or educational level, value system, communication style, religious beliefs, or ethnicity.

Even in our modern world, we still have tribes, or networks of human belonging. Today, we form our tribes based on our profession, educational background, favorite athletic teams, hobbies and passions, economic class, social life, political leanings, religious faith, ethnic heritage, and so on. But research tells us that those who have learned to live beyond the tribe, who have come to move smoothly among different networks of belonging, have a more sensitive way of seeing, understand multiple perspectives, and discover additional sources of strength to help sustain the Spirit that fuels our callings, commitments, and vocational challenges.[6]

Learning how to establish and maintain relationships with people of different personalities, cultures, and interests forces us to increase our interpersonal skills and sensitivities. Learning about the passions in the vocational work of others requires us to be students of another's trade. Learning how to move smoothly with members of another faith requires that we develop a clearer understanding of other religious beliefs, practices, and moral codes.

Living within just one core group can lead to a narrow sense of what's important, a limited sense of what's needed, and only one or two ways of coping with tough times. It is easy to remain fully immersed in one core group, but the resources of that one core group may easily reach their limit to sustain us through the complexities of today's vocational journey.

Multiple belongings helps us sustain the Spirit of our vocational choices in work, relationships, and faith because we become familiar with a greater number of ways to handle difficulties, communicate with others, appreciate what others cherish, and find meaning in what life brings us.

6. Marginality

Many of us can describe times in which we were ignored or pushed aside. No matter how humble, authentic, noble, or generous our vocational responses and commitments, we all face the possibility of being marginalized for one reason or another.

When it matters most, we may find that others push us to the margins where our opinions and talents are not considered. We may be marginalized because of our values, our convictions, our educational level, our financial status, our physical appearance, or even our geographic roots.

An exemplary principal who had ten years of success working with at-risk youth in an economically challenged urban high school was crushed when the school was forced to close. He accepted an offer to be the principal of a new, upper middle-class suburban high school. Of the experience, he said:

> In the suburbs, people either didn't know of my past success with kids, or didn't value it because "those were tough city kids and our kids are totally different". All of a sudden, everything I had accomplished didn't matter, didn't count, was irrelevant. It was like my whole life's work—my vocation—was forgotten. Never happened. I was terribly lonely for nearly two years.
>
> Then, a student died in a car accident. All these big football players started crying uncontrollably. No one knew what to do. I did! Suddenly, all my past experience came bursting out. I naturally knew exactly what to do. Ever since, my work here is seen differently.

Marginality, that lonesome, cold place of exclusion and insignificance, does not have to hamper our ability to sustain the

Spirit. It does not have to send us off looking for another response to our vocational calls.

The gift of marginality helps us develop empathetic connections with others. Resilient people use occasional experiences of marginalization to re-examine and reaffirm their core values, becoming more sensitive to the marginalization of others and a bit more comfortable living on the edge.[7]

7. Habits of Mind

Blessed assurance, constructive engagement with others, belonging to different groups, and marginality all can help us develop thinking habits that make it easier to see past simple solutions and easy answers. These experiences can make it easier for us to think beyond and below the obvious, and to connect the dots that contribute to certain problems and solutions.

These experiences cultivate *systemic* thinking instead of *simplistic* thinking. Those of us who want to "keep it simple" put ourselves at risk, because responding to the call of work, relationships, and faith today is increasingly complex. We can better sustain the Spirit when we cultivate our ability to get below the surface and see the multiple factors or benefits involved in a situation.

Those who sustain the Spirit have also learned to practice a kind of internal dialogue in which they seek different points of view with the hope of enhancing, but not compromising, their own.[8] Others fearlessly seek 360-degree feedback—not just feedback from a select few or those "in the loop," but from anyone who may have an impact on their response to the three vocational callings. As Mike Krzyzewski, a highly successful college coach, wrote:

> I'll frequently ask a variety of people how they see our team. What are our strengths and weaknesses? Do they see any problems? What do they think we need to work on? I may ask my secretary, our sports information director, or my wife questions like these. And I'll ask D.C., the person who cleans our locker room....

There have been a couple of times when I've been working in the locker room on something and D.C., who's been cleaning in the background, will pipe up with a comment. Leaders aren't the only people who can think of innovative things. Good ideas come from anywhere and everywhere. And often they come from the people you least expect to have them.

My mom was a cleaning woman. She was also the best person I've ever known. And she had all kinds of great ideas. So I figure that anybody in any job can have a good idea. Can a person who cleans the floor in your organization give you a suggestion? And more importantly, will you listen to that person?[9]

Developing these habits of mind allows us to cultivate richer resources for sustaining the Spirit. Through perspective-taking we find that balancing the dialogue between ourself and others helps us stay on our vocational feet. Through systemic thinking we gain insights that were previously hidden, we avoid the frustration of expecting an easy solution, and we develop increased patience with complexity. Practicing 360-degree feedback reminds us that everyone counts to some degree, including those we oppose and those we have placed on the margin.

8. Holding Contradictions

Most of us require clarity and consistency from the people around us. However, those who are comfortable with paradox, ambiguity, and contradiction appear to be better equipped to sustain the Spirit behind the callings, commitments, and vocational challenges of life.[10]

A young adult fresh out of graduate school with a Master's degree took a promising leadership position. His programs were outstanding. Participants were delighted. Numbers soared. Feedback from those served consistently reflected appreciation and gratitude for helpful information, sensitivity to the difficulties of their work tasks, and relevant suggestions. However, the recent graduate soon became increasingly disappointed with the politics, bureaucracy, and inconsistency of the corporate leaders. He resigned, saying, "It's too hypocritical. I can't be part of it! I told myself in graduate school that I would never be part of that!"

Three years later, when our paths crossed, he replayed his past experience. He said sadly, "What was I thinking? I was using my degree. We were offering excellent programs. The people were delighted...and no one was getting in our way! Now I'm doing something I don't really feel called to, does not reflect my interests, and only has a minimal level of success. But I can't afford to go back or start over because now I have two little kids."

The young man couldn't accept the contradictions that were part of his vocational call of work, and now he regretted it.

None of us should compromise our principles of integrity. To do so would put our vocational Spirit at risk. Compromising our deepest-held values and convictions will certainly kill the lifeline of passion and integrity fueling our vocational commitments. But before we get to the point of having to compromise our spiritual integrity, we may be pleasantly surprised to see that there may be far more room than we think to live among the paradoxes, ambiguities, and inconsistencies of our vocational commitments.

Vocational spirituality includes a deepening and growing capacity to accept the truth that we are all flawed. Some of us seem to be naturally capable of accepting this truth. But perhaps most of us, like the young college graduate, need years of maturing and seasoning in order to develop the capacity to fully accept contradictions. This means cultivating a tolerance for some ambiguity, an appreciation for paradox, and an eye for irony.

The human efforts, institutions, and interactions that we commit to and count on within the call of work, relationships, and faith will never be perfect. As part of sustaining the Spirit, we can each work at increasing our capacity for living with the complexities of human imperfection, and for keeping the contradictions in balance before prematurely terminating our commitments and callings.

9. Taboo Motivations

Vocational spirituality also includes cultivating the ability to handle our own human flaws, compulsions, and contradictions. Sustaining our vocational commitments doesn't require sainthood. It helps to take honest inventory of the motivations behind the commitments we make to work, relationships, and faith.

What motivates you most in the way you live out work relationships, and faith? The research of Daloz, Keen, Keen, and Parks found that people who sustain commitments to service reported being driven by "taboo motivations" such as ambition, perfectionism, and the desire to please people.[12] Instead of minimalizing, denying, or repressing the compulsive nature of their motives, those interviewed described their determination to accurately *name* their motivations, honestly *claim* the effects of their motivations, and engage in efforts to *tame* the power these taboo motivators had on them.

> Committed people work out of both the light and shadow of their lives.[11]
>
> —Daloz, Keen, Keen, & Parks

Anger is one of the most common taboo motivations, and is often described as a form of dissatisfaction that fuels action. As a community activist in Harlem relates: "I bless anger. It gets me out of bed in the morning to try to help people find what they need to survive." Anger is often described as the blue flame of fire that ignites the stove, the furnace, or the hot water heater. This flame is a necessary source of heat that has a positive function when regulated, but one that becomes dangerous and destructive if turned up too high.

Despite obvious dangers, some taboo motivations actually have upsides. Ambition unchecked is self-serving, ruthless, and dangerous. But to the extent that we name, claim, and tame it, ambition can motivate us to be successful in our work, relationships, and faith. The same can be said about perfectionism. Like the other taboo motivations, it can control our lives, burden us, and limit our ability to sustain our commitments. On the other hand, naming, claiming, and taming perfectionism can help us to maintain high standards for ourselves as we relate to others, do our work, and live as persons of faith.

Too often we are coached and counseled to dispel taboo motivations such as ambition, perfectionism, or the desire to please people. Those of us motivated by such things are told that we "have issues," or that we are "dysfunctional" or "co-dependent." It may very well be, however, that sustaining the Spirit of our vocational commitments includes staying aware of the mixed nature of our motivations and being responsible for the way we name, claim, and tame them.

10. Pain-fullness

Recent interest in vocational callings seems to be driven by the promise and pursuit of happiness. Psychologists who specialize in happiness and well-being have much to offer us as we seek to enhance the quality of our lives and the use of our time.

But vocational spirituality is really not about getting into a "flow" of happiness that comes from optimal moments. In fact, vocational spirituality is not really about the pursuit of happiness; it's more about the pursuit of purpose.

The vocational journey is less about happiness and more about living with some of the hard choices, sacrifices, and responsibilities found in responding to the three distinct but overlapping calls. Thus, vocational spirituality:

- is less about happiness and more about integrity;
- is less about happiness and more about faithfulness;
- is less about making ourselves happy and more about knowing for who and what we will stand up for, who and what we will commit to, and who and what we will put before ourselves;

When the experience of pain makes you more thoughtful

You measure your words
    more carefully.
When faced with a decision
    you ask who gets hurt.
When someone shines the light
    on your accomplishments
    you look in the shadows
    for the colleagues overlooked.

When the experience of pain makes you more thoughtful
You pay more attention.
Passion and compassion
    get married to each other.
You hear the cries of human desire
    uttered around you without words.

When the experience of pain makes you more thoughtful
You develop a tender strength
    and a strong tenderness.
You get weaker
You get wiser
You allow pain to touch you
    but not take hold of you.

When the experience of pain makes you more thoughtful
You find new ways of being
    sensitive and sensible
A thoughtfulness born from pain
Call it pain-fullness.

            —Michael Carotta

- is less about knowing how to make ourselves happy and more about knowing why we will keep our word, why we will light a candle instead of cursing the darkness, and why we can sing in the midst of grieving;

- is less about doing and more about hearing and seeing matters of the Spirit;

- is less about the pursuit of happiness and more about the experience of loving.

The loving experience of vocational commitments doesn't come coated in Teflon. We should not be shocked or disappointed to find that vocational commitments bring each and every one of us the pain of rejection, apathy, ridicule, loss, and even betrayal. But research reveals that instead of disowning painful vocational commitments, those who sustain the Spirit allow pain to touch them but refuse to get lost in it.[13]

Many people who are wounded by the pain that comes from their work, relationships, or faith appear to learn from it, and can often use it to recognize pain in others. We have decided to call this thoughtfulness born from pain "pain-fullness." This denotes an empathy that develops from one's own experience of heartache. Pain-fullness is a compassion shaped by one's own moments of suffering. It is insight and wisdom formed from one's own mistakes and confusion. Pain-fullness levels the playing field. It brings the right out of righteousness, and takes the judge out of judgment.

Cultivating pain-fullness is another trait of vocational spirituality. Pain can help us sustain the Spirit of our commitments if, from the struggle, we are better able to predict when our words may cause pain, when the spotlight shed on us may place others in the shadows, when some of our past patterns need to be changed, and when the vulnerability of others requires our tender strength and strong tenderness.

In her book, *My Grandfather's Blessings*, Rachel Naomi Remen describes the blessing of painful as "wrestling with the angel."

Sometimes a wound is the place where we encounter life for the first time, where we come to know its power and its ways. Wounded we may find a wisdom. That will enable us to live better than any knowledge and glimpse a view of ourselves and of life that is both true and unexpected....

How tempting to let the enemy go and flee. To put the struggle behind you as quickly as possible and get on with your life. Life might be easier then but far less genuine. Perhaps the wisdom lies in engaging in the life you have been given as fully and courageously as possible and not letting go until you find the unknown blessing that is in everything.[14]

11. Holy Urgency

"Passionate" is a word often used to describe those who are living out vocational commitments. Passion is the central element of the vocational life. Passion transforms a laborer into an artist, a believer into a disciple, a family member into a best friend, a colleague into a teammate, a spouse into a soulmate, a coach into a teacher, a leader into a learner.

Our passion makes it seem natural to overcome difficulties within our relationships, obstacles in our work, and moments of emptiness in our faith. Our passions help us endure unpleasant vocational seasons within each of our three vocational callings. Sometimes, advice such as, "calm down," "be patient," and "consider the big picture" actually serves to pour cold water on the passion fueling our vocational commitments.

And yet our unbridled passion can take us to extremes where we lose perspective and balance. Unbridled passion can become obsession, which diminishes empathy, makes big deals out of small matters, and puts our vocational commitments at risk. Therein lies the dance. Can we live with enough passion to fuel our commitments and still not be consumed by it?

Sustaining the Spirit within our commitments seems to require a curious mixture of humility *and* self-importance, perspective *and* passion. This is what is known as holy urgency.[16] Holy urgency is found in those who say "My contribution may not compare with all the other great works being accomplished, but it's the most important contribution I can make. I will stop at nothing to do it well, and I will not lower my expectations!"

Holy urgency is the balancing mechanism within vocational spirituality. By maintaining this holy urgency—this balance of humility and passion—in your vocational responses to work, relationships, and faith, you protect yourself from extremes of inferiority or superiority, passivity or overstatement, settling for

---

Nothing is more practical than finding God,

    that is,
    than falling in love
    in a quite absolute, final way.

What you are in love with,
    what seizes your imagination,
    will affect everything.
It will decide what will get you out of bed in the morning,
    what you will do with your evening,
    how you will spend your weekends,
    what you will read,
    who you know,
    what breaks your heart,
    and what amazes you with joy and gratitude.

Fall in love,
    stay in love,
    and it will decide everything.[15]

—Pedro Arrupe, SJ

less or delusions of grandeur, extremes which can extinguish the fire sustaining the Spirit of your commitments.

Holy urgency is also about the paradox of time. We know that something must be done *now*, while knowing that what is good and right happens over a long time of continued implementation. Holy urgency is the drive of immediacy tempered with recognition of the need for patience. It is planting now for a later harvest. It is the most important moment in a lifetime of other important moments.

Holy urgency challenges us to ask questions such as these: "What is the passion that fuels my commitment?" "When are my efforts really not that important?" "Why must I do this now?" and "What if I wait?"

12. The Passing Partner

The process of sustaining the Spirit in our callings, commitments, and vocational challenges requires each of us to have a partner, whether for a moment, a minute, a month, a year, or another amount of time. A passing partner is not someone we seek out and invite to join us for the journey of a lifetime. The passing partner is someone who mysteriously moves into our circle as if his or her orbit naturally intersected with ours; a partner planted more than planned; a partner for a season.

Passing partners have angelic functions. The ways this person thinks or listens, counsels or collaborates, is balm for our soul—and the passing partner probably doesn't even know it. In fact, we ourselves may not even be consciously aware of the effect that the passing partner is having on our ability to sustain some aspect of our commitments within work, relationships, and faith. (However, if you are lucky enough to realize it, you are obligated to say so.)

When sharing the idea of a passing partner with a group of colleagues in Richmond, Virginia, a friend named Dennis quickly responded "A certain musician was once my passing partner! I listened to his album every day on my way to work. That musician accompanied me through a tough time in my vocational life." Others in the group quickly identified their own passing partners. Someone explained that she had read several books by a certain author whose writings had carried her through a particular vocational season. Another described a time when a slogan had been a source of strength. Yet another described how a pet had served as a passing partner, and another brought forth a wave of laughter in describing the encouragement once found in a new (and perhaps faddish) "movement" now long gone.

The partner you are blessed with for one point in time might not be the same person or group that journeys with you through another. The person that helps you sustain the Spirit through one challenge may not be the same one who comes your way during the next challenge. Those you partner with during one monumental task may not be among those you partner with on the next one.

Don't try to hold on to a passing partner once that person's work is done, even if you still see him or her every day. The dynamic of the passing partner is another aspect of the mystery that makes up vocational spirituality. The partners along the way are given to us, sometimes in a temporary way, and sometimes against our grain and preferences. We do best to stay open to their possibilities and purpose for our journey.

13. Keeping Sabbath

Sustaining the Spirit of our commitments requires more than cultivating certain ways of thinking, living with complexity, or properly balancing our motivations. It requires more than turning pain into thoughtfulness or maintaining a holy urgency, more than interpersonal sensitivities and professional resources. Responding to the callings, commitments, and vocational challenges of your life also requires an intentional caring for the soul.

Keeping Sabbath is the practice of taking time for solitude, for introspection, for worship, and for rest. In a culture that requires multitasking and in which most of us feel overwhelmed, it is easy to lose sight of the values and virtues we hold most sacred. Many of us keep the Sabbath through traditional forms of worship within our faith communities. Some of us have our gardens, while others have our books. And some of us take some form of a Sunday morning walk.

> No culture dedicated to enchantment recognizes our need to live in a world of both facts and holy imagination. It understands that wisdom and deep intelligence require an honest appreciation of mystery.[17]
>
> —Thomas Moore

Keeping Sabbath enables us to pause long enough to evaluate what really matters, to examine our actions and interactions, restore our souls, and connect to the transcendent. Whether Muslim, Hindu, Christian, or Jew, intentionally keeping Sabbath through worship and rest helps us see the way our responses to the call of faith influence the way we are living out the call of work and the call of relationships.

Keeping Sabbath sets aside a time and place to see how our vocational callings and our everyday responses to them affect each other, whether in harmonious or acrimonious ways. More than anything else, the process of keeping Sabbath is a way of regaining vocational strength by restoring inner peace and right relationship, as well as fostering a sense of reconciliation and spiritual renewal.

For Reflection

1. What vocational season are you in right now—spring, summer, fall, or winter—within the following areas?
    — the call of work
    — the call of relationships
    — the call of faith

What is your current experience in each area that inspires you to assign this season?

2. What are the natural dimensions of your vocational roles and responses in each of these areas?
    — the call of work
    — the call of relationships
    — the call of faith

What can you do to enhance these natural dimensions without trying to eliminate them?

3. When and by whom were you given blessed assurance that you were trustworthy and capable of contributing to others? At this time, who might be counting on you to provide him or her with blessed assurance?

4. What experiences of engagement with others have influenced you most? How would you describe their influence on you? Rate yourself in terms of your natural tendency toward engagement with others.

1	2	3	4	5
Lone Ranger				Highly interactive

5. What are the different groups that you belong to? Describe what you learn from each of them. How have multiple belongings helped you sustain the Spirit that fuels your callings, commitments, and vocational challenges?

6. When have you experienced marginality? Has it helped or hindered your ability to sustain the Spirit?

7. Check the habit(s) of mind you would like to cultivate or improve:
   ___ situational analysis
   ___ dialogue
   ___ seeking feedback
   ___ perspective-taking

8. How well do you live with complexity? Accept contradiction? What are some of the complexities, contradictions, or human imperfections you are currently dealing with in the following commitments?
   — the call of work
   — the call of relationships
   — the call of faith

9. What taboo motivations fuel your commitments in:
   — the call of work
   — the call of relationships
   — the call of faith
Consider the effect each taboo motivation has on you, then think about ways to name, claim, and tame it.

10. What experience(s) have helped you develop a sense of painfullness? How and when do you demonstrate this?

11. How does your holy urgency show up in your vocational responses to each of the following?
   — the call of work
   — the call of relationships
   — the call of faith

What has been the cold water that has extinguished some of your passion? In what areas do you need to get your passion under control? When and how would you like to display a better sense of holy urgency?

12. When you review your vocational callings, commitments, and challenges who comes to mind as a passing partner? Who might list you as a passing partner on their vocational journey?

13. How can you improve the way you are intentionally keeping Sabbath?

Endnotes

1. Allen, James. *As a Man Thinketh*. Philadelphia: Running Press, 2001.
2. Daloz, Laurent, Cheryl Keen, James Keen, and Sharon Parks. *Common Fire: Leading Lives of Commitment in a Complex World.* Boston: Beacon Press, 1996. Nearly half of the thirteen elements described in Part 2 were derived and fashioned from this book.
3. Palmer, Parker. *A Hidden Wholeness: The Journey Toward An Undivided Life*. San Francisco: Jossey-Bass, 2004.
4. Daloz et al, *Common Fire*.
5. Ibid.
6. Ibid.
7. Ibid.
8. Ibid.
9. Krzyzewski, Mike and Donald Phillips. *Leading with the Heart*. New York: Warner Books, 2000.
10. Daloz et al, Common Fire.
11. Ibid.
12. Ibid.
13. Ibid.

14. Remen, Rachel Naomi. *My Grandfather's Blessings.* New York: Riverhead Books, 2000.
15. The Jesuits frequently use this quote from one of their own, Rev. Pedro Arrupe, when exploring and describing vocational callings.
16. Daloz et al, Common Fire.
17. Moore, Thomas. *The Re-Enchantment of Everyday Life.* New York: Harper Perennial, 1997.

Part 3

Challenges & Practices

*A*nd you, too, youthful reader, will realize the Vision (not the idle wish) of your heart, be it base or beautiful, or a mixture of both, for you will always gravitate toward that which you, secretly, most love. Into your hands will be placed the exact results of your own thoughts; you will receive that which you earn; no more, no less. Whatever your present environment may be, you will fall, remain, or rise with your thoughts, your Vision, your ideal. You will become as small as your controlling desire; as great as your dominant aspiration...."Gifts," powers, material, intellectual, and spiritual possessions are the fruits of effort; they are thoughts completed, objects accomplished, visions realized.

The Vision that you glorify in your mind, the Ideal that you enthrone in your heart—this you will build your life by, this you will become.[1]

—James Allen

*T*here are natural challenges all of us face as we live out our vocational responses to the calls of work, relationships, and faith. Some challenges are obvious and pressing, while others are quietly eroding our ability to sustain the Spirit. While some challenges come from the people and institutions we work with, live with, or believe in, others we inflict on ourselves. Within our responses to the calls of work, relationships, and faith, at least seven challenges seem to be common experiences that put our vocational lives at risk:

- Desensitization
- Superhuman Expectations
- Complexity
- Mediocrity
- Ethic of the Enemy
- The Fall of a Mentor
- Inequity and Injustice.

Let's take a look at each of these challenges.

Vocational Challenges

Desensitization

Desensitization is about becoming numb. It is about losing the ability to feel the needs of others. It is about no longer having the ears to hear the voices of human desire, which is the heartbeat of vocational living.

Human desire can be heard in a co-worker's ambitious plans for success, in her or his dedication to the details of the job, or in the fearful forecasting of unfavorable evaluations. It can be heard in the sound of children at play, in the intimate voice of loved ones, and in the tearful sobs of rejection. Human desire can be heard in the questions of seekers, the prayers of believers, and the songs of the congregation. It can be heard in the hum of daily tasks and events, in the way teenagers laugh freely with friends, and in the silence of a retreat to read in peace.

When desensitization sets in, we figuratively step over wounded colleagues on the way to the coffee pot. A teacher no longer hears the child crying in the playground as she or he heads to the car after school. A parent fails to notice the increasingly quiet resignation in the voice of a teenage son or daughter. We buy a ticket and sit in the stands, but we are unable to cheer for the team. We have no idea what vocational season we are in. We forget to ask a friend or relative about their doctor's appointment or job interview. We call our aging parents only once in awhile.

Desensitization is also about no longer using our "eyes to see" the spiritual nature and details of our vocational journey. It is about failing to hear the voice of God calling us in the silence of our hearts, as well as through those with whom we come in contact.

Desensitization challenges us from the environments of our vocational journeys: from places of apathy, indifference, preoccupations, obsessions, self-absorption, or the unconscious acceptance of suffering. Sometimes it comes from our own need to screen ourselves off from the experiences of others, or from fatigue. In our culture today, multitasking is no longer an exceptional skill pursued only by the extremely talented: it is now commonplace and required. The hectic pace of our lives, the noise of a media-driven culture, and the complex nature of post-modern opportunity can drown out the voice of human desire and obscure our ability to be aware of the spiritual dimensions of our lives and the lives of those around us.

Vocational spirituality is about walking on the sacred grounds of people's lives.[2] The vocational journey of respecting and responding to three different callings puts us in touch with the soulful longings and heartfelt dreams within ourself and within others. When we lose our "ears to hear and eyes to see" through desensitization, it's easy to forget why it's worth the effort to sustain our vocational commitments.

Superhuman Expectations

We live in a culture that places great value on that which fixes, solves, heals, corrects, prevents, protects, restores, or succeeds. Superhuman expectations within work, relationships, and faith can be nearly impossible to maintain.

The expectations within each of these three calls are seductive. We are seduced by achievement. If we could fix this, attend to that, help with this, and be responsible for that, then we could enjoy a good reputation and a greater sense of productivity. We are seduced by benevolence. The more we can accomplish, the more people will be served. Both simultaneously and at different times, we are expected to counsel and confront, give and take, lead and follow, teach and learn, work hard and relax, take risks and be careful, volunteer and stay home.

At a workshop recently, a participant responded to a discussion about the danger of buying into superhuman expectations: "I get it. You can spread yourself so wide that you end up being a big lake only one inch deep." The person paused a moment before adding, "And when you get to a vocational season of winter, you'll freeze up pretty quickly; and in the heat of vocational summer, you could dry up."

Superhuman responses within vocational calls seem to be expected. The modern call of work seems to expect both workmanship and leadership, quality and cost efficiency, long hours and sharp focus, compliance and creativity. The modern call of relationships seems to expect social skills and physical beauty, caring for others and caring for self, interdependence and independence. The modern call of faith seems to expect discipleship and fellowship, confidence and questions, prayer and action.

But overextending ourselves by trying to fulfill superhuman expectations of both this and that within work, relationships, or faith will rob us of our interpersonal, professional, and spiritual depth. Unless we adapt to the challenge of superhuman expectations, we set ourselves up for despair and ineffectiveness.

Most adults become partners in an intimate relationship they seek to sustain over many years. Most adults parent children. Most adults take up paid employment. Many adults pursue their own expansion through schooling or psychotherapy. All adults in contemporary America share citizenship with people whose skin color, gender, age, social position, sexual orientation, and physical condition differ from their own. These activities present us with a vast variety of expectations, prescriptions, claims, and demands....What these diverse claims have in common is this: they all require a degree of complexity that goes beyond the fourth order of consciousness...Nearly all of us are out of our depth when it comes to the "honors track" in our culture's curriculum: the mental burden of postmodernism.[3]

—Robert Kegan

Complexity

Science has given us new insights into the many differences we have in the way we best learn, handle emotions, and express ourselves. Technology brings us information in a minute and communication now requires new skills. We are more aware of our different religious beliefs and customs. Children fret, adolescents worry, adults look for meaning. Questions are tougher than they used to be, and the answers are no longer always easy.

Postmodern life is a layered and interrelated one.

- The call of work must now be answered within the complexity of diversity, individual ambitions, corporate goals, economic opportunity, and educational requirements.

- The call of relationships must now be answered within the complex tensions of self-sacrifice and fulfillment, individual interests and family responsibilities, security and self-expression, parenting and eldercare, airports and living rooms, e-mail and holiday visits, independence and interdependence.

- The call of faith must now be answered within the complexity of individual searching and denominational beliefs, flawed human nature and the Holy Spirit, ecumenical dialogue and religious fanaticism, interfaith marriages and same-sex unions, medical ethics and moral responsibilities, social justice and the global village.

This is the vocational challenge of complexity. It is harder and harder to know how to partner well, perform admirably, contribute, or accompany. The increased complexity of modernity can erode our ability to shift, evaluate, make adjustments, and keep growing. In the face of increased complexity, it is easy to move toward oversimplification, rigidity, frustration and detachment. Yet the research shared in the previous section on sustaining commitments suggests that vocational commitments require just the opposite kind of response.

Mediocrity

Of all the vocational challenges facing us, acceptance of mediocrity is the quietest *and* the most harmful of all. There is usually no great pain or trauma involved in accepting mediocrity. Unlike other adaptive challenges within our vocational callings, it is not a thorn in our side, or a burden we must bear. Accepting mediocrity is a gentle but deadly threat to our vocational callings and commitments.

Whether it is found within our work, relationships, or faith, the lullaby of mediocrity is the same: "It's good enough." This lullaby is sung in many different forms and has many different verses.

- Within the call of work, favorite forms of the lullaby are sung with excuses and advice such as "Bide Your Time," "Don't Make Waves," "That's The Way It Is (Deal With It)," "It's Out of Our Hands," and "Don't Take It So Seriously."

- Within the call of relationships, the lullaby of mediocrity can be heard in such phrases as "Chill Out," "It's Not Important," and "Things Could Be a Lot Worse."

- Within the call of faith, mediocrity is sung in traditional mottos such as "Let God Take Care of It," "God Understands," and "The Poor Will Be With Us Always."

All of the above lullabies contain empathic dimensions and can serve constructive purposes. But when played as a means of accepting mediocrity, these tunes only rock us to vocational sleep.

Mediocrity slowly extinguishes the blue flame sustaining the Spirit of our vocational passion by encouraging us to lower our standards. When we do this we place our vocational journey on the path of ineffectiveness, which leads us to apathy. This is a very dangerous place for our vocational spirit, because it can die there. Apathy makes the flame of vocational passion easy to blow out. It leaves us with little motivation to reignite the blue flame of passion.

Ethic of the Enemy

In some way, we are all involved in the creation of enemies. According to Christopher Bollas, we all use external objects as a way of articulating who we are and who we are not.[4] We appear to reap three psychological benefits from creating an ethic for the enemy: avoidance of responsibility, increased bonding with those in agreement, and identity clarification.[5]

- By unconsciously creating enemies, we have someone or something else to blame for our troubles, and thus avoid placing responsibility for a problem or a solution on our own shoulders.

- Second, we develop stronger bonds with colleagues, friends, or family members who are "on our side" because now it's "us" against "them" (the enemy).

- Third, we are better able to define who we are and what's important to us, because we can now point to the enemy and say with conviction "I'm not like *that*."

The enemy concept can be applied to individuals, classes of individuals, political systems, institutions, media, marketing campaigns, objects of frustration, and even elements of nature. We often make "isms" the enemy: racism, capitalism, feminism, liberalism, conservatism, communism, and pluralism. Cultural objects are easily made into enemies as well: illiteracy, criminality, poverty, illegitimacy, and diversity.

The language we use contributes to the enemy ethic. The linguistic construction of the enemy ethic can be found in the subtle use of "we" and "they," or more loaded words such as "attacking" someone else's view, "killing" off hope for a raise, "fighting" for approval of your plan, "owning" the situation, "dominating" the conversation, "controlling" the relationship, "forcing" the agenda, and "overcoming" lack of support.

We also contribute to the enemy ethic non-verbally via closed doors, raised eyebrows, exchanged looks hidden from a third party, and intentional non-communication. We whisper conversations, abruptly end others near the presence of "the enemy," or subtly ask a friend or colleague, "Did you survive the meeting?"

We make enemies out of family members, supervisors, politicians, bureaucrats, coworkers, theologians, columnists, talk show hosts, health care professionals, parents, children, and teens. Yet sustaining the Spirit that fuels our vocational callings and commitments is difficult enough without carrying the burden of animosity and tension on our backs and bitterness in our hearts.

Vocationally speaking, the ethic of the enemy is like kryptonite, the heavy and chemically charged rock that could rob Superman of his strength. Maintaining an ethic of the enemy is like carrying the heavy rock of kryptonite in your vocational backpack. It weighs us down and makes us less able to respond to the other challenges that put our vocational life at risk.

It is already hard enough to face the vocational challenges of desensitization, superhuman expectations, complexity, and mediocrity. The burden and tension found in maintaining an enemy ethic also prevents us from having the lightness of feet and the nimble ability to respond to the wind of the Spirit as it blows mysteriously through our vocational journey.

And like the radioactive kryptonite, the ethic of the enemy will spread from our vocational backpack and fill our insides with bitterness. If bitterness takes root within us, our vocational life will not survive without a major intervention.

Fall of a Mentor

With some of the previous vocational challenges, we are spread too thin. Other vocational challenges lead to exhaustion, apathy, confusion, bitterness, dullness, or loss of inspiration. Yet no other vocational challenge will bring us the pain of a broken heart like the fall of a mentor. The irony here is that this pain only breaks the heart of those who have already experienced wonderful mentoring, or those who maintain an ideal of mentoring.

Within the call of work, relationships, or faith, the experience and the dream of wonderful mentoring is filled with openness to new ideas, appreciation for thoughtful insights, mutual accountability, encouragement to try again despite failure, a willingness to take on new and worthwhile endeavors, gratitude for small, good things, a sense of the sacred, and a sense of humor.

We can be blessed by mentoring from a parent, a spouse, a friend, a spiritual director, teacher, coach, or a supervisor. Traveling the vocational journey of work, relationships, or faith with a mentor to help guide us is indeed a mountaintop experience.

Mentors fall for all sorts of reasons. Sometimes we put mentors on pedestals that are too high for anyone to maintain the esteem we place on him or her. Sometimes mentors move on, retire, or pass away; sometimes they mislead.

The fall of a mentor can also be experienced in the loss of a vision, a mission, or an ideal. These can sometimes lead us, shepherd us, and mentor us as wonderfully as any human being, and we may grieve their loss just as deeply.

After experiencing life-giving mentorship, we can become brokenhearted with emptiness and loss when our mentor falls. Gone is the companionship. Gone is the vision. Gone is the excitement of new adventures. Gone is the trust, the honesty, the possibilities, the energy, the credibility of that relationship. What might have served to mentor now seems to be a tormentor.

Experiencing the fall of a mentor often leaves us so disappointed and demoralized that we don't want to get out of our vocational bed. Unlike the other adaptive challenges noted in this chapter, the fall of a mentor can leave us in need of healing. It begets the question, how do we return to our vocational journey?

Inequity and Injustice

It has become more and more clear through our workshops and conversations that the pain and suffering brought on by injustice and inequity can be so pervasive and so deep that it can be nearly impossible to sustain our vocational callings and commitments.

We make and sustain our vocational commitments in work, relationships, and faith through self-sacrifice, hard work, integrity, and love. When we embrace the responsibilities of our vocational commitments in this way, we expect organizations, colleagues, family, friends, athletics, and religions to avoid intentional and ongoing practices that are unjust, destructive, or exploitative.

Sometimes we are wounded by the inequity and injustice experienced by friends, family, and colleagues within our vocational circles. Sometimes we ourselves are the victims of inequity and injustice. Inequity

> The very word "practice" brings with it the idea of learning. And any practice is awkward and difficult at first. But it is necessary to attain any kind of proficiency in the spiritual life.[6]
>
> —Dorothy Day

and injustice evoke in us a range of emotions: sadness, despair, anger, rage, resignation, and depression.

Inequity and injustice can have such a strong effect on us that we no longer wish to continue on the vocational journey within our current roles or commitments. We may quit jobs, change careers, terminate relationships, move away, or seek a different religious tradition. In order to move past or survive this kind of pain, we need the healing presence of friends, family, and colleagues who understand our vocational callings and commitments *as well as* our suffering.

The Power of Practice

We believe in the power of practice. Practices are deliberate ways of stepping toward a vocational challenge instead of trying to find ways of avoiding the challenge. Practices are intentional ways of doing something instead of simply trying to hold on. Practices are *proactive* responses instead of *reactive* ones.

> Practices are those shared activities that address fundamental human needs and that, woven together, form a way of life....Practices, therefore, have practical purposes: to heal, to shape communities, to discern....Practices possess standards of excellence....A practice has a certain internal feel and momentum...each practice is ever new, taking fresh form each day.[7]

Most practices require discipline, and some call for a certain way of thinking. Some require courage, and others call for a lot of heart. Some require finding "new eyes," while some require find "new ears." According to John Daido Loori:

> Ordinary understanding is seeing with the eye and hearing with the ear. Intimacy is seeing with the ear and hearing with the eye.[8]

When we begin to consciously engage in certain practices, we have a more active role in the way we sustain the Spirit of our vocational choices. The process of reviewing the challenges and re-imaging proactive ways of adapting to those challenges is really about realizing the authentic nature of our deepest self and fulfilling the "Promise to Become."

Consider the following practices as ways to proactively respond to the challenges that can put our vocational life at risk:

- Collecting Moments of Grace
- Remembering Who You Are
- Coming to the Balcony
- Testimony
- Confession
- Leading Without Authority
- Keeping Company.

Collecting Moments of Grace

All of us have been given a token of appreciation by someone who wanted to show how much they valued something we may have done for them. These objects represent concrete moments of grace when someone reverenced our effect on them.

Even though moments of grace themselves do not come in the form of a physical object or symbol, we can still collect them. In doing so, we exercise the spiritual nature of our three calls. Collecting moments of grace can be likened to deliberately tending to our spiritual lives as we do our gardens, noticing natural and spontaneous elements like a new bud, a graceful bird visitor, a threatening weed, or dangerously dry soil. The practice of collecting moments of grace is actually about paying attention.

> Paying attention is how we use our psychic energy, and how we use our psychic energy determines the kind of self we are cultivating, the kind of person we are learning to be. When we give our full attention to something, when we are really attending, we are calling forth all our resources of intelligence, feeling, and sensitivity.[9]
>
> —Robert Bellah

Paying attention is making a deliberate effort to put a name to a reality and then deciding what to do about it. It involves a conscious and intentional investment in the well-being of those we encounter.

The practice of paying attention is rooted in a sense of hopefulness and involves paying, or giving up, the energy to attend to what is present, what is missing, what is affected, what is assumed, what is broken, and what is possible. Paying attention in this way brings renewed spirit back to our vocational journey, carrying us out of the numbness and callousness of vocational fatigue and self-absorption.

There are at least four different moments of grace that we can collect within the daily experience of our call to work, relationships, and faith:

- Moments of "coming to know" are present in another's soulful longings, passions, dreams, or treasured interests. Collecting these moments depends on the generous self-disclosure of another and on our own ability to be trusted. Sometimes, someone may graciously yet subtly share something that his or her heart holds sacred, but we may be too caught up or distracted to collect it.

- Moments of reverencing the work are present when others stop to appreciate our work. Such moments usually come with a physical token of appreciation and are easy to catch. But they can also come in the form of a verbal compliment, a warm touch or embrace, or the grateful way a friend, family member, or colleague looks you in the eye.

- Moments of vulnerability remind us of the spiritual dimensions of life and occur when we see someone who is overwhelmed by a situation, distraught over an event, or unnerved by a task. Collecting the moments of grace found in vulnerability requires showing a strong tenderness and a tender strength.

The range of what we think and do
  is limited by what we fail to notice.
And because we fail to notice that we fail to notice,
  there is little we can do
  until we notice how
  failing to notice shapes our thoughts and deeds.[10]

—R.D. Laing

- Moments of re-enchantment with the ordinary can be captured when we realize the secret of the mystics, who kept their inner joy and sustained their Spirit throughout history, despite plagues, famines, inquisitions, and oppression. The secret of the mystics can be found in the belief that the present is sacred and the ordinary is holy.

When we treat the present as our best source of good things instead of racing through it because of what we must do tomorrow, we will find many moments of grace there. When we treat the ordinary as holy instead of the extraordinary, we will celebrate small successes, grieve over minor losses, and walk kindly through daily drama. Reminding ourselves that the present is sacred and the ordinary is holy may be the most powerful way to exercise our "ears to hear and eyes to see," the spiritual nature of our vocational callings.

Remembering Who You Are

Remembering who you are is the intentional practice of coming back inside yourself to reclaim and remember what you do best, what you care about the most, and what others saw in you when they first offered you the blessed assurance of your trustworthiness and capabilities.

Remembering who you are includes making sure that no matter what additional tasks and superhuman expectations may dismember us within relationships, work, or faith, we can fiercely hold on to the tasks that come most naturally to us. In this way, we are able to preserve and protect our sources of joy and fulfillment. It is the practice of dreaming to be something more while knowing exactly who we are.

> You need only claim the events of your life to make yourself yours. When you truly possess all you have been and done, which may take some time, you are fierce with reality.[11]
>
> —Florida Scot-Maxwell

The practice of remembering who you are in the face of vocational challenges is about staying faithful to our natural inheritance, that is, our innate talents, passions, and values. It must also include remembering our dream, that soulful vision of how we imagine ourselves coming into who we are.

Remembering who you are includes remembering who and what we respect and love. It is remembering to have a conversation with ourself about ourself. It is the practice of remembering what is true and of coming to terms with our limitations.

The practice of remembering who you are can help you distinguish the voices of human need from the noise of bureaucratic systems and institutional agendas. Remembering who you are is a way to recover your moral compass within the dizzying experience of trying to fulfill superhuman expectations, resist the pull of mediocrity, navigate through complexity, and stay on your chosen vocational journey.

> The struggle to be something more than the person others have made, to construct and then live up to a set of our own expectations, is one of the most compelling struggles of our adult life.[12]
>
> —Laurent Daloz

Remembering who you are includes taking time to remember those people who were instrumental in helping you hear and respond to your vocational call of work, relationships, or faith. By connecting with those influential others, we re-establish a strong sense of connectedness and history within our vocational story, something that is often lost or forgotten as we deal with superhuman expectations.

Coming to the Balcony

Ronald Heifetz proposes that the practice of coming to the balcony means occasionally rising above the dance floor in order to get a better view of the dynamics, interactions, pace, and other fac-

> Engaged in the dance, it is nearly impossible to get a sense of the patterns made by everyone on the floor. Motion makes observation difficult. Indeed, we often get carried away by the dance. Our attention is carried away by the music, our partner, and the need to sense the dancing space of others nearby to stay off their toes. To discern the larger pattern on the dance floor—to see who is dancing with whom, in what groups, in what location, and who is sitting out which kind of dance—we have to stop moving and get to the balcony.[14]
>
> —Robert Heifetz

tors making up the complexity of our vocational dance.[13] Coming to the balcony enables us to gain a view we cannot obtain while we are on the dance floor itself because the view on the dance floor is obscured by the complex movement of the other dancers.

The practice of coming to the balcony is about intentionally taking time to be a critical thinker and a reflective practitioner. Some of us practice it on a regular basis, while others do so only occasionally. Some of us practice coming to the balcony in a structured way, while others do so via informal conversations whenever such moments present themselves. And some of us can practice coming to the balcony while the dancing and the drama is still going on, as if running up the steps for a quick and analytical view on our way to the rest room.

Engaging in the practice of coming to the balcony involves pausing to name issues and to accept contradictions. It can be a way to develop habits of mind much as dialogue, systemic thinking, 360-degree feedback, and perspective-taking. Often it is best to take a confidant with us, someone who has clear eyes and a straight tongue.

Margaret Guider, OSF, of the Weston Jesuit School of Theology, encourages us seek the "wisdom of the ratio" when coming to the balcony.[15] This concept is found in determining the ratio of "how much" to "when," instead of choosing one approach over the other. For example:

- How much understanding is needed? When has there been too much?
- When should I confront? When should I console?
- How much do I need to control and how much do I need to let go?
- How much clutch and how much gas?
- When should I speak up and when should I shut up?
- How much should I reveal and how much should I keep to myself?
- How much should I speed things up or slow things down?
- When should I accept things as they are and when should I never accept things as they are?
- When should I consult with him and when should I consult with her?
- How much should I address and how much should I ignore?
- How much energy should I invest in this and how much should I invest in that?
- When and how should I balance actuality with potentiality? Duality with mutuality? Individuality with commonality?

We can practice coming to the balcony and seeking the "wisdom of the ratio" as we address the vocational challenges making up the dance and drama of our work, relationships, and faith.

Testimony

In response to mediocrity's dangerous lullaby of "It's Good Enough," testimony is the courageous practice of making a public statement, whether to one person or to twenty-one, with words or with actions that say, "It's *not* good enough for me."

> The practice of testimony requires a person to commit voice and body to telling of the truth. In testimony, people speak truthfully about what they have experienced and seen, offering it to the community for the edification of all.[16]
>
> —Dorothy Bass

The practice of testimony is about deciding to be excellent in large and small matters. Even if we don't know how to improve a situation, truthfully testifying that something "is not good enough" strengthens the fire to sustain the Spirit, fueling our callings and commitments, keeping us off the path of ineffectiveness and apathy. In the midst of experiencing injustice and inequity, the practice of testimony is our way of speaking truth to power.

The courageous practice of testimony is the public naming of what is best, noble, acceptable, or true. Again, it is important to note that we can practice testimony with words or with actions before one person or a group of one hundred and one persons.

Testimony may also be the one practice we can do for the edification of others. When others struggle with the vocational challenge of complexity, our testimony can help them as they come to the balcony to sort things out. When others come to us disheartened by inequity or injustice, our testimony can remind them of why their efforts are still worth it. When others come to you lost in superhuman expectations, our testimony about their natural talents and the core values we have seen them demonstrate can help them remember who they are.

The practice of testimony is about making decisions regarding the quality of our relationships, work, and faith so as to remain an author in the story of our own vocational journey. But testimony is different from all the other practices. Collecting moments of grace, remembering who you are, and coming to the balcony all require intentionality and discipline of thought. Testimony, however, requires courage and a heart.

Confession

While the other practices consist of mental and interpersonal exercises, the practice of confession is an exercise of the soul. When engaging in the practice of confession, we go inward to do the hard work of admitting our biases, fears, insecurities, mistrust, contradictions, and convenient generalizations.

Like testimony, the practice of confession is a courageous one. It can take place in many forms and at many different depths. It can be a simple admission resulting from reflection, or it can be a more thorough moral inventory.

Confession enables us to let go of the ethic of the enemy and freely make the vocational journey without being burdened by the tension of animosity or poison of bitterness. It can lead us to reconsider or terminate some relationships, make new resolutions, and renew our commitments. It can help us own up to our acceptance of mediocrity in our work, relationships, and faith.

Confession also calls for humility. It should include an examination of our vocational conscience and apologies or reparations when necessary. When carried out with integrity, it will almost always liberate us to travel the vocational journey with a lighter heart and a clearer conscience, making it easier to collect moments of grace and adapt to the vocational challenges found along the way.

Human existence cannot be silent,
nor can it be nourished by false words,
but only true words,
with which [women and] men
transform the world.

To exist, humanly, is to name the world
and change it.

Once named, the world in its turn
reappears to the namers as a problem
and requires new naming.

[Women and] Men are not
built in silence,
but in a word,
in work,
in action/reflection.[17]

—Paolo Freire

Leading Without Authority

Leading without authority can be an appropriate way to respond to specific vocational challenges such as complexity, mediocrity, and the fall of a mentor.

Leading without authority is a proactive way to move forward through the web of complexity, the apathy of mediocrity, or the absence of guidance. It is a practice that realizes all of us take a turn at failing, inertia, lethargy, or neglect. It a practice that acknowledges that while one may be the right person to lead at a particular moment, that same person may be the wrong one to lead without authority in the next.

The practice of leading without authority will help us re-engage with our callings and commitments when we learn from the pain of failure or betrayal and demonstrate a true amount of pain-fullness to those frozen by complexity, asleep in mediocrity, or disheartened by a loss of leadership.

In his book, *Leadership Without Easy Answers*, Ronald Heifetz explains leading without authority in the face of complexity, mediocrity, or failure consist of three dynamics:

1. You decide which initiative or task to pursue. Choose the initiative that truly meets needs and the one you are most interested in.

2. You choose consultants. Instead of the normal consultation process with those "in the loop," you can now choose to consult with those "on the margins," or those without authority, or those closest to the task. In other words, you can disregard titles, roles, or relationships.

3. Thirdly, listen to the creative whisper inside you that begs you to do pursue the task in a creative way, even if it's a bit unconventional.[18]

Two words of caution: within the call of relationships, work, or faith, we should choose an initiative that authentically needs attention, not just one that will make us look good. When leading without authority, we can't expect support since we were never given authority. Nevertheless, this practice can be a timely and viable response to some of the vocational challenges that appear within our call to work, relationships, and faith.

Keeping Company

Vocational challenges can cause us to lose heart. In the midst of certain company, we come to believe that human goodness and the grace of God provides enough light for all of us to make our way past human imperfection and inequity. In the midst of certain company, we experience what it is we most believe in. In the midst of certain company, we taste what it is we hold most sacred.

We tend to let our relationships and networks develop naturally from the tasks and rhythms of our life. However, the long journey of sustaining the Spirit is best made when we intentionally practice keeping company with those who provide understanding, affirmation, affection, and a dose of confrontation when needed.

The practice of keeping company requires the ongoing and deliberate investment of our time, energy, and money into certain relationships. It requires that we block out time to visit with those we want in our company. It means calling someone up just to check in

---

When we lose heart,
Our Innocence becomes Cynicism
   and we dress it up as Realism.
Our Curiosity becomes Arrogance
and we dress it up as Authoritative Knowledge.
Our Compassion becomes Callousness
and we dress it up as the thick-skin of Experience. [19]

—Robert Heifetz & Martin Linsky

on him or her. It asks that we take the initiative in inviting someone out for a cup of coffee. It means honoring annual gatherings and cultivating rituals with those whose company we want to keep.

Keeping company is also about "venturing and abiding." Sharon Parks maintains that sustaining our vocational commitments is a process of *venturing* out into the world of our vocational callings, testing ourselves, making discoveries, and coming back to *abide* long enough to tell the stories.[20]

As we keep company, we find ways to tell our stories of inequity and injustice, superhuman expectations, and our own desensitization as they occur on our vocational journey. Even more importantly, in keeping company we find friends who understand our lamentations yet still assure us that we should continue venturing forth. Keeping company helps us to not lose heart.

In addition to investing the time, money, and effort needed for keeping company, we also need to exercise prudence. Not everyone belongs in our company. We must be selective as to the type of persons and personalities we wish to keep company with. Dr. Lorraine Monroe, known for her ability in educational leadership, advises that we not keep company with anyone who envies, complains, and drains.[21]

It is absolutely true that belonging to different groups of people whose views and values are diverse and opposing to ours can help us understand multiple perspectives and accept contradictions. By the same token, keeping company with those whose core values and hearts are not like ours will not help us in times of injustice and inequity. Sustaining the Spirit in times of injustice and inequity requires keeping company with those who both comfort and challenge us. Some of their voices cheer us on with unconditional support. Others ask us to re-evaluate, make adjustments, and stretch. The various characters in the company we keep may not even know or see each other.

By intentionally keeping company with mystics *and* managers, cheerleaders *and* prophets, dreamers *and* doers, the reverent *and* the irreverent, athletes *and* artists, cooks *and* corporates, coaches *and* clothes horses, we maintain a kind of eclectic and maybe even invisible community that never fails to offer solidarity, providing us with all forms of a tender strength and a strong tenderness.

For Reflection

1. On a scale of 1-10, with 10 being high, how would you rate your level of desensitization in the following areas?

___ work

___ relationships

___ faith

2. What superhuman expectations are eroding your ability to sustain the Spirit?

3. What are some of the complexities, particularly complex issues and complex times, that you are dealing with in your responses to the call of the following?

___ work

___ relationships

___ faith

4. Where in these three callings are you accepting mediocrity?

___ work

___ relationships

___ faith

5. How do you currently contribute to the ethic of the enemy? What emotions may be behind this? How can you stop contributing to or participating in this ethic?

6. Is there someone with whom you might want to build a bridge, mend a fence, or forgive? With whom or what might it be best to simply "shake the dust from your feet" and move on?

7. How have you been disheartened by the fall of a mentor?

8. What inequities and injustices make it hardest for you to continue with your vocational commitments?

9. When you look back over the past few weeks or months, how have you experienced these moments of grace?
   ___ coming to know
   ___ reverence for your work
   ___ vulnerability
   ___ re-enchantment with the ordinary

10. To whom or what should you begin paying attention? Specifically, how can you do so?

11. Which of your natural talents, interests, and values do you need to remember and reclaim? Who do you need or want to remember with? What did they see in you, or help you discover about your vocational callings?

12. What is the soulful dream that first captured your imagination and fueled some of your vocational commitments?

13. How can you practice coming to the balcony? Who would you like to take with you?

14. Over what issue(s) do you need to seek the wisdom of the ratio?

15. Over what issue(s) might you need to practice testimony? What words or actions will this require?

16. In which of the three callings might you want to practice confession?

    ___ work

    ___ relationships

    ___ faith

17. When have you practiced or witnessed someone leading without authority? What did you learn from it?

18. When have you witnessed someone successfully leading without authority? In what way(s) did it bring healing?

19. When have you witnessed someone poorly leading without authority? It what way(s) did it make things worse?

20. Is there any need for you to lead without authority now? If so, in which of the three calls?

    ___ work

    ___ relationships

    ___ faith

21. Take a minute to list those with whom you are intentionally keeping company. How do you practice keeping company with them? How has the experience of keeping company with them helped you to keep heart?

Endnotes

1. Allen, James. *As a Man Thinketh*. Philadelphia: Running Press, 2001.

2. Groome, Thomas. *Educating for Life: A Spiritual Vision for Every Teacher and Parent*. New York: Crossroad Publishing Co., 1998.

3. Kegan, Robert. *In Over our Heads: The Mental Demands of Modern Life* Cambridge, MA: Harvard University Press, 1994.

4. Godwin, R. "On the Function of Enemies: The Articulation and Containment of the Unthought Self." *The Journal of Psychohistory*, 22 (1994), 79-102.

5. Middents, G. Psychological "Perspectives on Enemy-Making." *Psychology: A Journal Of Human Behavior*, 27 (1990) 53-58.

6. Day, Dorothy. "On Pilgrimage," *Catholic Worker*, February 1953.

7. Bass, Dorothy, ed. *Practicing Our Faith: A Way of Life for A Searching People*. San Francisco: Jossey-Bass, 1997.

8. Loori, John Daido. *The Zen of Creativity: Creating Your Artistic Life*. New York: Ballantine Books, 2004.

9. Bellah, Robert, Richard Madsen, William M. Sullivan, Ann Swidler, and Steven M. Tipton. *The Good Society*. New York: Vintage Book, 1991.

10. Laing, R.D. *Divided Self*. New York: Viking Press, 1991.

11. Scot-Maxwell, Florida. *The Measure of My Days*. New York: Penguin USA, 2000.

12. Daloz, Laurent. *Mentor: Guiding the Journey of Adult Learners*. San Francisco: Jossey-Bass, 1999.

13. Heifetz, Robert. *Leadership Without Easy Answers*. Cambridge, MA: Belknap Press, 1994.

14. Ibid.

15. Dr. Margaret Guider, OSF, shared this image in a presentation she gave during the Teaching for Spiritual Growth Summer Institute hosted by the Weston School of Theology in Cambridge, Massachusetts, in 1995.

16. Hoyt, Thomas, in Dorothy Bass, editor. *Practicing Our Faith: A Way of Life for A Searching People*. San Francisco: Jossey-Bass, 1997.

17. Freire, Paolo. "The Catholic University: Reflections on Its Tasks." *Union Seminary Quarterly Review*, 47 (1993), 197-201.

18. Heifetz, *Leadership Without Easy Answers.*

19. Heifetz, Robert and Martin Linsky. *Leadership on the Line: Staying Alive Through the Dangers of Leading.* Boston: Harvard Business School Press, 2002.

20. Parks, Sharon. "Home and Pilgrimage; Metaphors for Personal and Social Transformation." *Soundings,* Winter 1989, 298-315.

21. Monroe, Lorraine. *Nothing's Impossible: Leadership Lessons: Inside and Outside the Classroom.* New York: Times Books, 1997.

Summary

The Promise to Become

*D*ream lofty dreams, and as you dream, so shall you become. Your Vision is the Promise of what you shall one day be; your Ideal is the prophecy of what you shall at last unveil. The greatest achievement was at first and for a time a dream. The oak sleeps in the acorn; the bird waits in the egg; and in the highest vision of the soul a waking angel stirs. Dreams are the seedlings of realities.[1]

—James Allen

*V*ocational spirituality involves soulfully responding to each and all three vocational calls, sustaining the commitments we make to these calls, and adapting to the challenges that put our vocational lives at risk. Here is what we've learned about vocational spirituality:

- Vocational spirituality is a journey. But it isn't a painless or easy journey.

- Vocational discernment is a two-step dance; that is, identifying which of the three calls are being sounded and from where: the voice of God from outside us, from within us, and in others. Discerning the call is essentially a spiritual practice of prayer.

- Vocational spirituality can be risky. You place yourself and your commitments in plain sight before friends, family, colleagues, supervisors, God, and everyone.

- Vocational spirituality includes cultivating the ability to handle our own human flaws, compulsions, and contradictions.

- Vocational spirituality includes a deepening and growing capacity to accept the truth of who we are and who we are not.

- Vocational spirituality is not really about the pursuit of happiness; it's more about the experience of loving. It's less about happiness and more about having "eyes to see and ears to hear." Vocational spirituality is all about your life, but *not* about a life that's all yours.

- Vocational spirituality is approached with a sense of curiosity, and it requires that we come to fully accept Mystery without ever getting fully comfortable doing so.

- Our vocations "come to life"[2] as we respond to the call we discern from the voice of God from outside us, from within us, and in others. It is the cyclical process of "venturing and abiding"[3] wherein we respond to the opportunities and responsibilities found in the call of work, relationships, and faith. Every so often we return "home" to share stories and to evaluate the congruence of our responses with the vision contained in our "Promise to Become."

- Vocational spirituality is all about determining how well a role within work, relationships, and faith aligns with our soul.[4] It is about noticing when the role needs adjustment, and when we may need to adjust the way we care for the soul.

- Vocational spirituality is, by its nature, a private matter. Walk gently and respectfully in vocational conversations and decisions.

- Sustaining a vocational spirituality is an intentional endeavor requiring discipline and the use of certain practices, some of which are thoughtful and some of which are courageous.

- Sustaining the Spirit is something we do both alone and together.[5] It is the constant adventure of addressing matters related to one call while being conscious of the effect such efforts may be having on each of the other two calls. It is living with and through the times that one call is hurt by the responsibilities and commitments we maintain in another call.

The three vocational calls of work, relationships, and faith invite all of us on a common journey and destination to fulfill our soulful dream and heartfelt "Promise to Become." Sustaining the Spirit in these matters and in these ways is really the Work of Our Life.

Perhaps now it is easier to see that vocational spirituality is not reserved just for those who have accepted the call to ministry or public service. It is alive in each person committed to the faithful, fearless, and authentic pursuit of *who* we are and *whose* we are.

May grace be with you as you respond to the call to fulfill your "Promise to Become."

Endnotes

1. Allen, James. *As a Man Thinketh*. Philadelphia: Running Press, 2001

2. Hansen, David. *The Call to Teach*. New York: Teacher's College Press, 1995.

3. Parks, Sharon. "Home and Pilgrimage; Metaphors for Personal and Social Transformation." *Soundings*, Winter 1989, 298-315.

4. Palmer, Parker. *The Courage to Teach: Exploring the Inner Landscape of a Teacher's Life*. San Francisco: Jossey-Bass, 1998.

5. Ibid.

Appendix

Circle the topics you wish to revisit or cultivate as you continue responding to the callings, commitments, and vocational challenges comprising the Work of Your Life.